# A FEW KEYS FROM THE PILE

Inspirational Keys to Living a

God Directed Life

By

Gayle M. Nelson

# A FEW KEYS FROM THE PILE

Inspirational Keys to Living a
God Directed Life

By
Gayle M. Nelson

*A Few Keys From the Pile:Inspirational Keys to Living a God Directed Life* is © 2013 Gayle M. Nelson

First Edition

Published 2013 by Gayle M. Nelson

No part of this book may be reproduced or transmitted in any form or by any means, electronic, mechanical, including photocopying, recording, or by any information storage and retrieval system, without written permission from the author.

All rights reserved.

Printed in the United States of America

Scripture quotations taken from the New American Standard Bible®, Copyright © 1960, 1962, 1963, 1968, 1971, 1972, 1973, 1975, 1977, 1995 by The Lockman Foundation Used by permission. (www.Lockman.org)

Scripture taken from The Message. Copyright © 1993, 1994, 1995, 1996, 2000, 2001, 2002. Used by permission of NavPress Publishing Group.

I am happy to dedicate this book to my husband. Living with me, loving and caring for me have not always been easy. His faithfulness deeply humbles me and I am grateful to the Lord for giving me a man as honorable as Wade Nelson.

# CONTENTS

|  | Pg # |
|---|---|
| Forward by Wade H. Nelson | 8 |
| Introduction | 10 |
| Why Keys? Why Dreams? Why Visions? | 12 |

**Section 1**
    PERSONAL ATTITUDE ADJUSTMENTS — 22

| | |
|---|---|
| The Key of His Cross | 22 |
| The Key of Real Passion | 28 |
| The Key of Rest | 33 |
| The Key of Letting Your Heart Take Courage – Hope | 36 |
| One Trial – Four Keys | 38 |
|   1. The Key of Freedom from Self Pity | 39 |
|   2. The Key of Repairing the Breach | 42 |
|   3. The Key of Momentary Light Affliction | 44 |
|   4. The Key of Tearing Down and Rebuilding | 46 |
| The Key of the Word Being a Ladder | 50 |
| The Key of Repenting of Blindness | 53 |
| The Key of Death First then Life | 56 |
| The Key of Asking Permission to Speak | 60 |
| The Key of the Weight of Sin | 62 |
| The Key of Playing with the Father | 63 |
| The Key of Faith vs. His Sovereignty | 65 |
| The Key of a Name Change Equaling a Character Change | 70 |
| The Key of Miracles | 73 |

**Section 2**
    FIGHTING THE GOOD FIGHT — 78

| | |
|---|---|
| The Key of Fighting the Spirit of Suicide | 79 |
| The Key of the Value of Intercession | 83 |
| The Key of Truth | 87 |
| The Key of Awesome Spiritual Warfare | 91 |
| The Key of Seeing through Somebody Else's Eyes | 93 |
| The Key of Team Work | 96 |

The Key of Puzzle Pieces                98

Section 3
    ATTITUDE ADJUSTMENTS
    NEEDED REGARDING OTHERS 103

The Key of Dissonance                  108
The Key of Reaping a Better Crop       111
Pizza Dream???                         113
The Key of Being a King Maker          115
The Key of Eating the Scroll           119
The Key of the Weight of False
Expectations                           120
The Key of Getting in the Game         122
The Key of a Whirlwind / Twister / Storm   124

Section 4
    LESSONS THAT ARE BIGGER
    THAN ME                       128

The Key of Getting Out of Jail         128
The Key of the True Power of Mercy     131
The Key of Extracting the Precious
from the Worthless                     132
The Key of God's Approval              135
The Key of Seeing the 'Light'          138
The Key of Taking Time to
Change Our Minds                       144
The Key of Knowing the Times           147
The Key of Being a True Worshipper     152
The Key of the Living Fountain         155

CONCLUSION                             158

Many Gifts and Countless Keys          158

## **Forward**

Christians are called pilgrims, sojourners, ambassadors, all words describing people who have no permanent home. Here is one pilgrim's take on that journey. Gayle has captured that tension between living in this world and longing for a better home with our Lord. She calls us to a deeper, less superficial walk; where God is truly first, and there is more to life than just getting by here on earth. She calls us to live in eternity NOW; it is not something we have to wait for.

She longs to be fully clothed "with our heavenly dwelling", as II Cor 5:2 states. Verses 4 and following captures her heart and attitude well: "For while we are in this tent, we groan, and are burdened, because we do not wish to be unclothed but to be clothed with our heavenly dwelling, so that what is mortal may be swallowed up by life. Now it is God who has made us for this very purpose and has given us the Spirit as a deposit, guaranteeing what is to come. Therefore we are always confident and know that as long as we are at home in the body we are away from the Lord. We live by faith, not by sight."

Her one true desire is to know God more intimately, to walk with Him more closely and to enjoy His presence. Along with this, she wants others to enjoy this same intimacy with God, and this book is about that journey.

She is totally committed to the truth, and as a result you will find her to be brutally honest, but first with and about herself. II Cor 13: 5 states: "Examine yourselves to see whether you are in the faith; test yourselves." Her life is an example of this, constantly re-examining her positions and opinions to make sure she is in harmony with her Lord. And she has changed over the years. It takes some effort at times to convince her she is wrong, but when she comes to that realization, she jumps in with both feet, freely abandoning long-held beliefs and attitudes that are now a source of hindrance.

As an example of this changing, in the previous paragraph I used the term "brutally honest", which is not quite accurate anymore. She is still totally committed to the truth, but it is no longer used as a weapon. That is the biggest change I have seen in her, that she has not lost the ability to cut through all the nonsense and get to the heart of a matter quickly, but can now deliver the message in a way that it can be received for positive growth.

Keep this in mind as you read of her journey, being ready yourself to change, to grow, to get to know our Lord better and deeper. This is not a how-to guide as much as a personal diary, as you get to observe one pilgrim's progress, hopefully gaining some insight in how to change your own life. She reveals the inner workings of her journey, and the sometimes painful changes that needed to occur for her to realize her goal of closer intimacy with her Lord.

So sit back, enjoy, and be ready to examine your own life, to clear away those hindrances that keep us from a deeper walk.

*A Few Keys From the Pile*

## **Introduction**

I HATE CAR TROUBLE! A while back, I was having difficulty starting my car. When I put the key in the ignition it didn't always start. Sometimes I could start it with one turn of the key. Other times it might take twenty turns. My husband and I weren't sure if it was the starter or the key itself that was the problem. Then one day, I tried to unlock the car door and it wouldn't open until I tried several times. I realized then that the problem was the key. It was worn down and nearly unusable.

I purchased new keys at the car dealership. So, problem solved, right? NOPE!

As I drove away from the car dealership I heard the Lord whisper to me, "I have given you several **keys** that you have ignored. It's time to gather them, write them down and distribute them."

Keys…what keys?

The Lord uses many different ways to train us…sometimes we can be unaware of His leading. We think it's merely common sense or something that we have just figured out ourselves. But these timely experiences are keys to growth and freedom…if we will only see His leading, guiding us or pushing toward His plan for our lives.

I went home from the car dealership and got a journal and started to record every lesson the Lord has taught me that I could remember. Afterwards, I documented on the computer the stories around the lessons, or 'keys', He had given me. When I was finished, I gave it to my husband to read and edit. He started asking me questions. "How did I know…?" "What does that mean?" "Would you elaborate on it please?"

Then my very wise husband said, "Gayle, you're going to have to write what it cost you to learn these things. You're going to have to write about the personal application or these stories don't mean anything. You need to expose yourself in this book or there's no point in writing it!"

Its funny how the Lord works, isn't it?

It turns out that we had to get a new starter for the car, but the ineffectiveness of the keys is what started this journey. In the same way, I was satisfied with simply writing the keys and leaving it up to the reader to find their own application, but God wanted more. In both things, the car keys and the lesson keys, I would have settled for the least. But God always requires more. He wants more of our hearts, more of our trust and more of us to mold into His vision.

The keys were the lure into a deeper process.

This book is really just about <u>spiritual</u> common sense. But, after years of leadership and counseling, I am aware that common sense, whether spiritual or not, isn't always common.

These Keys are questions the Lord longs for us to ask…and allows Him to answer in His own way and timing. He is whispering questions to you even as you read this book. Will we turn down the noise of our lives to hear His still small voice the way John did as leaned he against His chest…listening to His heart beat… The Lord waits for us to listen to Him as John did.

Do we have the courage to ask the questions…to turn the keys and see what lies beyond the door?

I believe that we all have been given 'Key' lessons throughout our lives. But we are unaware of them. We just keep moving through life without realizing that these lessons are not just beneficial to us but can be very helpful to others as well. My greatest hope as I write my 'Key' lessons down is that you will come to the understanding that you have many 'Key' lessons too! I hope you will stop to consider how the things God has taught you can bring understanding to those around you. And, maybe selfishly, I hope to somehow hear of the wisdom the Lord has given you in your life lessons. We are a community…we are meant to share and encourage each other.

## Why Keys? Why Dreams? Why Visions?

The Master Creator has a specific design for our lives. His artistry is obvious in light of the natural beauty all around us. Even our bodies speak to the wisdom of His masterpiece and workmanship: our intricately functioning systems; how we are formed; how we reproduce; our natural healing process.

And consider how He teaches us. We are instructed as though each of us is in a classroom of one with One mentor giving each of us individual attention. He is skilled beyond words, patient over and above measure with inscrutable wisdom. If we but learn to yield to His guidance we can tap into His limitlessness.

He often has chosen to teach me through dreams and visions. The dream that begins this book writing journey is as follows.

## The KEY Dream:

Many years ago, I had a dream about keys. In this dream, a man in black pants, white short-sleeved shirt and a black bow tie ran up to me with a big smile on his face. He looked like a gas station attendant from the 50's coming to wash my windshield, check the tires or do some other service on my car. He stood in front of me with one hand on his hip and the other hand extended and holding an old fashioned round, black Rolodex. I asked him what he wanted. But he just stood there smiling, arm extended, and seemed to want me to take the Rolodex. So I reached for it and as I did, it opened and many many keys spilled out onto the ground between us. I asked him what these keys were for, but he didn't speak, he just continued to smile. Soon a pile of keys began to grow. And after a little while (I don't know how long) the pile was almost as tall as I was. When the pile was so high that I could no longer see the man with the Rolodex, I woke up.

## The Instruction Begins:

I almost always think that my dreams are 'pizza' dreams, which means that they have absolutely no spiritual significance. But when the Lord speaks in dreams, He usually talks to me about the dream when I'm awake. He began to impress on me that I needed to start examining and collecting keys.

After this dream, He often drew me into discussions about these keys. What kind of keys are they? What did He want to unlock? Through the years I have often pondered what these keys are for. Keys to the kingdom? Keys to people's hearts? Keys to mysteries? Keys to the future? As I continue to ask the Lord what He wants to open, I can see that the possible uses for this myriad keys are endless.

When I had the key problem with my car (in the introduction) the Lord impressed on me that now was the time to gather the keys and list them. To be perfectly honest, I wasn't even aware that I had any keys at all. I was just living my life. But the Lord seemed to put a title to each lesson He taught me. Each time He gave me understanding, it was a key that unlocked a door to Him I hadn't noticed before. Every key was an opportunity to know Him better. How could I resist turning them?

In this book, you will see that much of what the Lord shows me is visual. Sometimes He speaks to me through dreams and visions. I have often thought He had to speak to me that way because I wasn't as intellectual as some people who can learn by studying His written word alone. I have always admired people like my husband, who is very smart. He understands and seems to dig into the Word of God and can serve it to the body of Christ. He can find revelation in the most obscure passages. Those things tend to fly right over my head. So I have sometimes felt a little foolish having to learn through dreams and visions. But when He speaks to me in that way, I can't forget what I have seen and I MUST KNOW MORE. I have to know what He is trying to tell me and what He is requiring of me.

A friend of mine wishes that the Lord would speak to her through visions and dreams. It sounds so exciting to her. But I've always enjoyed listening to her churn up wisdom from the reservoir of deep water from her family heritage in God and revelations of the Word. I guess we as humans wish for what we don't have.

I believe we learn and function according to the gifts the Lord gives us. This is the way that He chooses to teach me. He may teach you in a different way. One way of learning is not necessarily better than another… just different.

Since these dreams and visions come under the heading of prophetic insights, maybe I should start this book by giving you some understanding into how I see prophetic words. There are two main thoughts that I have when it comes to prophesy.

1.) I believe the Lord desires to communicate with us all the time. He speaks through His word, worship, prayer and through supernatural as well as common ways. I think that He wants us to want to hear and speak to and for Him, as this is a benefit to ourselves as well as His body. He wants us to be available and willing to serve Him as we seek Him.

1 Cor 14:1
Pursue love, yet **desire** earnestly spiritual gifts, but especially **that you may prophesy**.

1 Cor 14:3-4
But **one who prophesies speaks to men for edification and exhortation and consolation**.
One who speaks in a tongue edifies himself; but one who prophesies edifies the church.

2.) Not everything that we hear in our spirits is the Lord speaking. Jeremiah 23 is a terrifying chapter of scripture for anyone who hopes to hear from the Lord. I have included a few of the verses, but much of that chapter frightens me to my bones. If you are not familiar with that chapter, I have added some of it below.

Jer 23:28-32
28 "The prophet who has a dream may relate his dream, but let him who has My word speak My word in truth. What does straw have in common with grain?" declares the LORD.
29 "Is not My word like fire?" declares the LORD, "and like a hammer to shatter rock?"
30 "Therefore behold, I am against the prophets," declares the LORD, "who steal My words from each other."
31 **"Behold, I am against the prophets," declares the LORD, "who use their tongues and declare, 'The Lord declares.'**
32 "Behold, I am against those who have prophesied false dreams," declares the LORD, "and related them, and led My people astray by their

falsehoods and reckless boasting; yet I did not send them or command them, nor do they furnish this people the slightest benefit," declares the LORD.

I should take a moment here to explain why Jeremiah 23 frightens me so much. I consider that passage as part of God's perspective on the prophetic. It reveals how the Lord 'feels' about true and false 'words'. In Jer.23 the Lord discloses how angry it makes Him when we cheapen and make insignificant the very Word of God. <u>If we aspire to speak for Him, the fear of the Lord is not only important, it is critical for ourselves and the rest of the body.</u> Too much familiarity with God and too little concern for the Truth is an offense to Him. We must be more careful with His reputation and the goals that **He** wants to accomplish

> Frankly, I am amazed that more people are not afraid to claim that they speak for the God of the universe.

With our very lives we speak for Him. You and I may be the only Christian or representative of the Lord that some people will ever know. We need to take the responsibility of representing Him accurately more seriously than we often do.

It is all too easy to add ourselves to the 'word'. But when we add what we think or how we feel we dilute His Word. <u>Diluting the Word of God with our humanness is much worse than making a mistake…In doing so we put our thoughts on an equal level with His thoughts, which (in my opinion) is the ultimate arrogance!</u>

As I wrote this book, my husband said about a million times, "Expand, explain, give me more of how you feel about this lesson. What does it mean to you?" Each time he asked me to expand the 'key' I had a hard time doing it. Because adding my feelings to God's lesson felt like I was cheapening His message. I want understanding to come, but I didn't want to be guilty of diluting His word. I hope that I have made a compromise between the two extremes of saying too little and too much. I have tried to reveal the process by which the Lord has taught me different 'key' lessons. I am trying to walk that tight rope of being transparent without diluting his message. I hope that you will see the balance.

God isn't playing around with His word. We **must let Him teach us to**

**properly fear Him**...fearing Him enough to give His words the weight that they deserve. And we can do that in a few simple ways.

1. By asking permission before speaking
2. By not adding our thoughts to His words
3. By waiting for his perfect timing.

The three above reference a few of the keys that I have learned and will be expanding on later.

One of my favorite scriptures is Rom. 11:22a "Behold the kindness and severity of God…" God is both kind and severe all of the time! Let's look at Heb. 10:26-39 and try to see the balance He makes between His grace and justice.

Hebrews 10:26-39
26   For if we go on sinning willfully after receiving the knowledge of the truth, there no longer remains a sacrifice for sins,
27   but a **terrifying expectation of judgment** and THE FURY OF A FIRE WHICH WILL CONSUME THE ADVERSARIES.
28   Anyone who has set aside the Law of Moses dies without mercy on *the testimony of* two or three witnesses.
29   How much **severer punishment do you think he will deserve who has trampled under foot the Son of God**, and has regarded as unclean the blood of the covenant by which he was sanctified, and has insulted the Spirit of grace?
30   For we know Him who said, "VENGEANCE IS MINE, I WILL REPAY." And again, "THE LORD WILL JUDGE HIS PEOPLE."
31   It is a **terrifying thing to fall into the hands of the living God**.
**32**   But remember the former days, when, after being enlightened, you endured a great conflict of sufferings,
33   partly by being made a public spectacle through reproaches and tribulations, and partly by becoming sharers with those who were so treated.
34   For you showed sympathy to the prisoners and accepted joyfully the seizure of your property, knowing that you have for yourselves a better possession and a lasting one.
35   Therefore, **do not throw away your confidence, which has a great reward**.
36   For you have need of endurance, so that when you have done the will of God, you may receive what was promised.

37   FOR YET IN A VERY LITTLE WHILE,
HE WHO IS COMING WILL COME, AND WILL NOT DELAY.
38    BUT MY RIGHTEOUS ONE SHALL LIVE BY FAITH;
AND IF HE SHRINKS BACK, MY SOUL HAS NO PLEASURE IN HIM.
39    **But we are not of those who shrink back to destruction, but of those who have faith to the preserving of the soul**.

Ok....if we practice 'sinning willfully', we can have an 'expectation of judgment' (vs.27). If we 'set aside the Law and insult His Spirit of grace' by choosing sin over obedience', 'severe punishment' awaits (vs.29). V 31 tells us that it is a terrifying thing to fall into the hands of the Living God! But at the same moment **we have the freedom to boldly come before the throne of grace** because of His sacrifice, Heb. 4:16. And we are instructed to 'hang onto this confidence' (vs35) and refuse to shrink back holding fast to our 'faith to preserve our souls'.

When I exhort you/me to be afraid...be very afraid to dilute the Word of God with your/my humanness, I am simply trying to pull both His kindness (GRACE) and His severity (JUSTICE) together. Yes He loves you and me more deeply than we could ever comprehend. Yes He lived, suffered and died so that we could live. Yes His sacrifice completely covers all of our sin. AND yes we must fear and reverence Him as GOD! Yes we must prove by our words and actions that His Word weighs more than ours. Yes we must begin with the fear of the Lord if we hope to learn any wisdom.

Eph. 3:17-19
17  so that  Christ may dwell in your hearts through faith; *and* that you, being rooted and grounded in love,
18  may be able to comprehend with  all the saints what is the breadth and length and height and depth,
19  and **to know the love of Christ which surpasses knowledge**, that you may be filled up to all the fullness of God.

Ps 111:10
10  The **fear of the LORD is the beginning of wisdom**;
A  good understanding have all those who do *His commandments;*
His praise endures forever.

It's confession time!  You may have noticed that I lean toward the severity of God more than toward His grace. Leaning too far in either direction is inaccurate and obviously not the full counsel of God. It is my belief that more times than not, Christians lean too far in the direction of grace. My caution is that we are not so full of His grace that we lose respect for His Holy Word, or that we are so lacking in faith that we are afraid to deliver His Word. The truth is that His love does cast away all fear and that the fear of the Lord is the beginning of wisdom.

It is a narrow path; each extreme is fraught with danger. On one side we may fall into presumption if we assume that every thing we hear is "of the Lord". And on the other, we may fall into faithlessness if we choose to shrink back from His calling us forward into His will. We must learn to strike that balance within His kindness-grace and His severity-justice. Whether this balance is defined as a narrow path or a tight rope, we are responsible to represent His heart.

I am regularly blown away by His mercy, grace and love toward me. I would not be as forgiving or patient as He. I am often critical and narrow in my thoughts. I usually don't look or act like my Dad. But still He draws me closer. Still He claims me as His daughter and loves me more that I can comprehend. I don't understand His love and gentleness toward all of us. I want to represent Him as the loving Father that He is. But He is wholly righteous, perfect and my Lord; not only my savior, my master; and I choose to be His bond slave. I believe that we should treat Him with great honor, obedience and yes, holy fear because He is GOD!

I will take a moment here to explain what I mean by bond slave. A bond slave in ancient Israel was a person who owed a debt and had entered into an agreement to work off the debt. In the seventh year, that slave or worker was free to go home. But if he chose to align himself to his master, then he was making the choice to work to prosper that master. This slave has become a bond slave because he gave up his freedom to become a part of the master's household. Therefore, as a Christian, I am not living for myself anymore. I live to please my Lord and He can do with me what He wills. I belong to him; these are not idle words, they are my chosen lifestyle.

While it is a narrow way, His hands are big enough to catch us and set us right again! Maybe we are our own worst enemy. We are often standing in His way! We ask Him to use us…allow us to be a conduit for His mercy, power and grace, and then we block up the hose with fear, sin or faithlessness. We have to get out of His way and trust Him to move through us like fresh water. He wants us to take a step and then another on the tight rope of faith. He loves us so He is ever the patient teacher. So we can step out in faith while at the same moment yielding to His holiness so that we don't step off into presumption and offend Him.

.Matt 16:19
"I will give you the **keys of the kingdom** of heaven; and whatever you shall bind on earth shall be bound in heaven, and whatever you shall loose on earth shall be loosed in heaven."

Keys bind and loose. The Lord also uses these keys to unlock and lock too. He is asking us to be responsible with the 'power' that He freely gives us. I believe He would have us release people from the bondage of judgment. By forgiving those who have wounded us, we are choosing to release them.

Keys are very small things that can open up a whole new world. We get to choose whether we will turn the key. Will we open up to the Lord, and by doing so, bring heaven to earth. God chooses to work through us. He requires us to be involved. God does not allow the evil on earth to happen for some greater purpose. NO! He moves through our prayers of faith… so in a way you could say that we are the ones that allow awful things to happen. We choose not to turn the key of prayer. What an extraordinary responsibility we have. To take the authority He has already given to us and watch the Lord pour forth the kingdom of heaven right here on earth!

Amos 3:7
Surely the Lord <u>GOD does nothing Unless He reveals His secret counsel To His servants the prophets.</u>

From the scripture above we see that God does reveal His plan to His servants. He reveals His secrets to us. If we are called by Him to be His mouth to the world, we must prove worthy of that honor. A wise person reveals secrets to those who can be trusted. The Lord trusts us with Himself…His very Word. We can honor Him by being trustworthy and by allowing Him to dictate the terms of sharing what He has to say.

I was telling one of my friends about writing this book about keys. She started to laugh and said, "Well, it's about time!" She reminded me of a word that was given to me at a prayer meeting for a legislator and me. The word was about having keys and using them.

Rev 3:7-8
7 "And to the angel of the church in Philadelphia write: He who is holy, who is true, **who has the <u>key of David</u>, who opens and no one will shut, and who shuts and no one opens**, says this:
8 'I know your deeds. Behold, **I have put before you an open door which no one can shut**, because you have a little power, and have kept My word, and have not denied My name.

There was more to the word, but she told me that after that word was given, every time she prayed for me the Lord would remind her of the 'keys'. So, I guess it's time to do a little 'key' exploring.

I hope you enjoy reading these 'keys' I have gathered. I also hope that you will consider what keys the Lord has given you for the good of His body.

I'm going to be honest and very forthright about my experiences. The Lord teaches all of us through our trials and stumbling. So, <u>throughout this book, you will see me using the key of transparency</u>. I didn't give transparency a key of its own because it is the thread woven though every key. If we hope to be guided or guide others into growth, we must make a commitment to be transparent. Being a see-through Christian is a powerful weapon against the enemy. The devil likes it when we hide and pretend that we don't have '*that*' problem.

When we keep the truth a secret, the enemy can isolate us. If we comply with his plan, we can't get the help that we need…and we are of little help to anyone else.

If you have a difficult time with being so open, let me give you an example of how the Lord changed my mind on the subject of transparency.

When I was growing up, my mom and I didn't have a very good relationship. I didn't respect her. She seemed very weak to me and I didn't want to be like her. My mom wore her heart on her sleeve. I remember being shocked on a regular basis by her complete openness with just about everything in her life.

As I grew older, I realized that she was much stronger than I was. She was real! I hid everything from everyone. I didn't want to appear to be weak, so I hardened my heart at every turn. All I accomplished was to make people think that I had no feelings at all. So, they could hurt me without guilt...after all I didn't feel it anyway. But that was of course a lie. And I caused my own heart to suffer for it.

Being open or naked with your feelings and your personal truths is much more difficult than hiding from them. When we are real, we are vulnerable.

The Lord revealed to me that if I want to be trusted, I have to be REAL!

So, lets get started turning some of those keys.

## Section I

## **PERSONAL ATTITUDE ADJUSTMENTS**

This first group of 'Keys' is about areas of my life where I needed an attitude adjustment regarding my personal walk with the Lord.

Sometimes we walk through life thinking that we 'know' something when we may have just heard it or read it. Until we can successfully and consistently LIVE it, we don't truly KNOW it! I think these key lessons the Lord imparted to me were His way of helping me 'know' and successfully 'live' these truths. I continue to grow in my understanding of these 'key' lessons and I hope that learning continues for my whole life-time.

## **THE KEY OF HIS CROSS**

Galatians 6:14 (NASB95)

But may it never be that **I would boast, except in the cross of our Lord Jesus Christ, through which the world has been crucified to me, and to the world.**
And when I came to you, brethren, I did not come with superiority of speech or of wisdom, proclaiming to you the testimony of God.
For **I determined to know nothing among you except Jesus Christ, and Him crucified.**

I will begin with the 'key' of His Cross because, though it is the last one that the Lord gave me for this book, it is the most important to me.

An illness called Lupus has allowed me on several occasions to learn valuable lessons through physical suffering. When I get past the, "Poor me" stage, I see these difficult times as 'opportunities' because the Lord is always faithful to turn each of them to good. So, though the enemy has tried literally to kill, steal and destroy, the Lord has caused all these things to bring Him glory.

I will refer to Lupus several times in this book, so I will give you a little

## Gayle M. Nelson

back-ground on Lupus and my struggle with it. I have been beaten up by it for most of my life. It is an auto-immune disease that is basically the opposite of AIDS, only weaker. Instead of having <u>too weak</u> of an immune system, mine is <u>too strong</u>. It's kind of like being allergic to yourself. My body is at war within. And I have battled in this war more times than I care to remember.

This first 'key' describes one such battle and the message of grace that the Lord helped me to receive.

At the end of October, 2005, I felt the Lord was leading me to press in for the healing He has already purchased for me at the cross. After thirty years of hoping, this message was both scary and exciting, scary because I have believed and been disappointed many times; exciting, because it seemed like the healing might finally happen. So I pressed in. Gradually, I felt led to increase my faith and prove my trust in Him by decreasing my many medications.

By decreasing the drugs, I was risking my life. I didn't do that out of presumption but because I believed the Lord wanted me to trust Him for this miracle. For a few months I experienced a freedom I had not known physically. Then, imperceptibly at first, my health began to decline. Within a month, I was incapacitated with pain. I took up residence in the 'land of denial' (place in my mind where this sickness had no hold over me) for a week or two. I wanted to be free so badly that I thought that if I could just believe, then I could truly experience total healing. But my health continued to decline. So reluctantly, after being bed-ridden for several days, I went back on the meds.

I had thought that maybe I hadn't been healed previously because there was a deficiency in my faith. I have been told that many times by Christians who couldn't reconcile why the Lord hadn't healed me. It was easier for them to blame me for a lack of faith then to try to understand that faith in the absence of His rescue is still faith. Their blame cost them nothing. They made me feel bad to make them selves feel better. It's so much easier to blame the person who is still suffering than to recognize that God can't be put in a box. He is not a trained rat. He does not do what we think He should because we do A, B and C. If they are correct and I am still suffering because of sin, then why isn't everybody sick?

In response, I committed myself wholly to believing that He had indeed already healed me. I left no room for any doubt. Faith can be a risky proposition. After I finally went back on the meds, my doctors questioned my sanity; "Were you trying to kill yourself?" they asked.

Depression doesn't even begin to describe how deeply disappointed I felt. I began to question whether I had heard His voice at all. I was also very angry with the Lord. I believe He has already provided for my healing... so what was the delay? Why was my hope yet again deferred?

When the Lord promises us something, we can trust that He will fulfill His Word. But we don't get to choose the circumstances of how He does it. He has promised us healing many times in scripture. But will it happen today or next year? Will I close my eyes to this world one night and wake up in His and then receive the completion of that promise? I don't know. I can't know for sure. But isn't that exactly what faith is: to believe in the absence of evidence? My body, mind and spirit are very frail so I have to lean on Him. No, I choose to lean on Him.

Believing what we as Christians believe does make us peculiar people, especially to the world, and in particular, the medical community. Though I felt that I was standing on the firm foundation of His Word, to the doctors, I appeared to be standing in the surf as the tide was going out, with the sand disappearing below my feet. How was I to explain my faith to doctors holding the grim test results in their hands?

Isaiah 59:1 (NASB95)
**Behold, the Lord's hand is not so short that it cannot save; Nor is His ear so dull that it cannot hear.**

Since I believe the Lord is able and has already provided healing with salvation, I came to the conclusion that He simply must not be willing. I wanted to rise above the disappointment, but had done so for thirty years and I guess I was too tired to get up quickly again. So, I turned away from Him and in my arrogance, I judged Him as not being good to me. I became a spoiled child, looking up at her daddy and pouting because I didn't get what I wanted.

For three weeks, I held onto the anger and disappointment. I didn't read my Bible, answer the phone, pray or receive prayer. I was resentful, disappointed, hopeless and hard-hearted.

Two weeks into this pity party I was throwing for myself, the Lord asked me to do something. Each time I went into my living room, the Lord asked me to look at a plaque that I had made and hung on the wall. It is a piece of rough wood, painted flat black with a cross made of steal rods with various metal wires wrapped around the cross. On it written in silver paint is: The Cross of Christ PROVES He is GOOD!

I originally made this piece of art to remind me that He is always good… even when the physical pain seems like more than I can take. I needed to have an ever-present reminder for my own heart and mind, like a seat belt to keep me safe when I felt like I was losing control and might crash into the wall of faithlessness.

For that whole week, I looked at that plaque every time I entered the room. In my head, I agreed with it…but my heart could not embrace it. I had lost the will to rise above my experience…to lift my vision higher than my circumstances. Yes, He is good…but I wanted to 'feel' His kindness…not just 'know' it in my head. I wanted to 'feel' His compassion. But I felt my heart hardening and I wasn't sure how to stop that process.

At the end of the third week, the Lord told me to sit down on the couch and meditate on what the statement, 'The Cross of Christ Proves He is Good', meant. I sat there for two minutes. Then I got up to leave and the Lord spoke so clearly to my heart: "**NO!**" He yelled inside of my head: "**SIT!**" I felt like a dog being commanded by her master to SIT! I felt that I was being punished. **I HAD BELIEVED HIM. I HAD HELD UP MY END OF THE BARGAIN! WHERE WAS GOD?** Furthermore, **I made that stupid plaque; I obviously knew what it said!** Why should I have to SIT there and meditate on what it meant??? But when God is that forceful in His command, what else could I do? So, I SAT and stared at the cross.

After about fifteen minutes of silence, I brazenly said to the Lord, "I'm not going to sit here all day! Speak something, or I'm leaving!"

Then the most amazingly strange thing happened.

In my spirit I heard Jesus talking quietly to the Father. It was His last day on earth. And it seemed I was eavesdropping on their conversation some two thousand years before. Was I hearing God…or was I just hearing voices like the crazy person the doctors suspected that I was? The conversation went something like this:

"Good morning Dad. Well, I'm the first to wake up…as usual. Today is going to be so hard. Soon they'll wake up and we'll go get something to eat and start our day…this last day with my best friends. But even though I'll be with them, it's going to be so lonely because they never really understand…they just don't seem to get it! And I'll explain what has to happen today to dull and unbelieving ears. Dad, I know one day they will see and understand what has to happen today, but right now that seems like a small comfort. Why don't they get it? Why is their vision so dim? I love them but they really frustrate me. And today will be a very long day."

I thought to myself: 'Does God talk like that? Do **I** frustrate Him like that? Is this what He was thinking that fateful morning? I thought Jesus had only 'holy' thoughts…was He really frustrated with them?'

The dialogue continued, "We'll spend the day together but not as 'ONE'. They will fight about petty things, like who is the greatest one among them, as if that even matters. I'll invite them to dinner, and I'll humble myself to them first and then to the world…and they still won't get it. I'll be betrayed by my best friends…abandoned and ultimately forsaken by You…the only One who really understands what's happening today. And even when I ask them to pray with me, their own weakness will overcome them. Oh Father, strengthen me! I need You! Help me to be defenseless. Help me to die so that they can live."

"Today is going to be my worst day here, Dad. **But my worst day will be their best day**. And even though they almost never get it…I look forward to giving myself up for them…so <u>one day WE will be ONE with them</u>."

Then I heard a different voice. It was the voice of the Father. In His wisdom He said to me, **"My Son's worst day was <u>your</u> best day. But you sit there on your couch and <u>you judge My Son as not being good</u>. YOU…YOU JUDGE MY SON! Why don't <u>you</u> ever seem to get it?"**

I suddenly realized that He was right…**I was '*judging*' Him** because I felt that He was unfair to me.

26

And just as suddenly, I understood how little I want 'fairness'. Because it isn't fair that He, the only sinless man, should die for me. It isn't fair that **He** should pay for my sin. It isn't fair that I was not grateful. It isn't fair that I, someone deserving death and hell, should receive life and heaven.

"Oh God, don't give me what I deserve!! DON'T GIVE ME WHAT IS FAIR!"

Psalms 103:10,11
He has **not** dealt with us according to our sins,
Nor rewarded us according to our iniquities.
For as high as the heavens are above the earth,
So great is His lovingkindness toward those who fear Him (NASB)

**He doesn't treat us as our sins deserve**,
 nor pay us back in full for our wrongs.
 As high as heaven is over the earth,
 so strong is his love to those who fear him. (same vs. Message)

**The cross of Christ does PROVE that He is GOOD!**

Yet almost every day we judge Him as not being good:...When our children choose to turn away from the Lord...When our marriages fall apart... When we get sick and the doctors tell us there is no cure...When our dreams of ministries don't happen the way we hoped that they would, when our hopes are deferred yet again.

The Father looks into our hearts and He hears our cries. We do matter to Him and He cares...but at the same time He whispers to our hearts... "Do you really think that I am not good? Do you believe Jesus died for nothing? Don't you understand that We would really rather die than live without you? Hasn't the willing death of My only Son proved that to you? Don't you realize your value to Me is immeasurable? **You were worth the blood of My own Son.**"

When I consider that My heavenly Father chose to sacrifice His own Son...and that to Him, I was worth Jesus' blood...I'm embarrassed about the insecurity that still remains in my heart. The God of the universe gave up His own life so I...we could live. HE IS GOOD! And He proved to us

He not only loves us, but that we truly matter to Him. I don't know about you, but I'm grateful. And now when I look at the plaque still hangs on my living room wall…my head not only knows He is good…but I choose to LET my heart FEEL it too. And when I fall and judge Him again…I will try to look up and see His cross.

## **THE KEY OF REAL PASSION**

The word passion describes an intense, overpowering emotion. I chose it to be one of the first keys because my personal passion to know the Lord and have fellowship with Him is a driving force in my life.

When I consider the word passion, four things come to mind. The first is the passion I have for my husband. He is perfect for me. His wisdom fills in my many blank spaces. His vision is well rounded and comprehensive. Most of the time I find myself feeling both blessed and lucky. Blessed that he is an obvious provision from the Lord and lucky I realized it. The Lord blesses me daily by giving me this man that loves me enough to lay down his life for me while he protects and makes a way for me. And I'm lucky because he values who I am and how the Lord uses me. The Lord has made us a team and we love moving, working and growing together. He is my best friend, the love of my life and together we three are one.

Next, I think of the kind of passion that goes into a call of God on our lives. Recently Wade and I went to a fund-raiser for India Partners. Two friends, Cliff and Colleen, were presenting information about the ministry as well as an opportunity to help. Abandoned, destitute girls litter the landscape in India. They are often forced into prostitution at a very early age. They are helpless and hopeless. India Partners offers many of these girls a place to live, eat and learn a trade so they can live a better life. This ministry brings the hope of God into their lives.

While I do believe that this is a valuable ministry, my heart was not drawn to jump in headfirst. But as I listened to these two friends, my heart was broken for these desperate girls. Colleen read the Dr. Seuss story, 'Horton Hears a Who'. If you haven't read it, let me take a moment to bring you up to speed. Horton (an elephant) hears a whole civilization of unknown people in a tiny speck of dust or lint. They are so tiny they could not be seen or heard without great effort. The whole book is about Horton's passion to get those around him to know what he knew. If he was not successful, all of these seemingly insignificant people would die. As I listened to her, I realized that she was Horton for these abandoned, seemingly insignificant girls.

Then Cliff began to tell us just a little bit about these individual girls. As he spoke, his heart was breaking for them. He gave these girls faces and names. I could see that the 'cause' didn't break him…his deep concern for each girl broke him. Everyone listening was trying not to cry. As a result, most people jumped in headfirst.

PASSION IS CREDIBLE! I read a book when I was lobbying at our states capital. It was called, "You are the Message". It was about how YOU are the reason anyone listens or ignores a story, proposition or a sales pitch. Your passion for any product, enterprise or position is the most important point…without passion you might as well not even start speaking. By credibility I mean, the **passion** that we have for anything but particularly for the Lord **WILL draw others**. It's not about being a great speaker. It's about having a heart of passionate longing for the Lord that lights a holy fire in us and through us coming directly from the Lord. I don't know how exactly to stir it up. I do know, however, that it is possible!

II Tim. 1:6 For this reason I remind you to **kindle afresh** the gift of God which is in you through the laying on of my hands.

The third thing that comes to my mind when I think about passion is the violence that causes some people to explode. They seem to be filled to the brim with anger, pain and a passionate bitterness that spills out whenever they are bumped like a tea cup filled too high. I think these people are greatly wounded, but instead of getting healed they choose to lash out. Anger and violence is so much cheaper than healing and forgiveness. <u>Allowing the Lord to heal us is very expensive</u>. When we choose to forgive, we must throw away our perceived right to live without restraint. **We don't get to be hateful and blame everybody for our lot in life**. We must lay aside our excuses for being bitter and forgive instead. We must put away our need to defend or protect ourselves. It is too expensive for some people. Angry people get to control those around them through fear and intimidation. So everyone else pays instead of the person who holds on to the wound. Remaining wounded and bitter is a cowardly way of living. When I wrote earlier about being hard hearted, not real, I think that I was living this false passion. I was a pretender. So nobody could really know me because I was hiding out of fear…attempting to protect myself. I was trying to appear to be strong when I was really very weak.

Lastly, I am reminded of the cross. ..the passion of our Lord and Savior. The time of suffering between the end of the Last Supper and the end of His life is known as the Passion. From the garden where He experienced great anguish…to being arrested, humiliated, stripped, whipped within an inch of His life, to carrying the cross bar of His instrument of death. His flesh then nailed to that cruel cross.

Flesh and nails shouldn't be in the same sentence, should they?

Then hanging up there naked, rejected and weighted down with my sin and yours. Then ultimately rejected and abandoned by His own Dad. He was lonely beyond any human means of description. Only great passion could drive Him to sacrifice so much.

I just had to know more about that passion, even though I was convinced that the cost would overwhelm me.

Back then in my private search to understand, I noticed a growing focus of the church was the truths within the Song of Solomon. I remember reading and studying this book a lot. However, many things eluded me. The portion below really bugged me because I lacked understanding. You could say it became an irritation in my heart and mind. It was a burr under my saddle, so to speak.

Song 8:6
"Put me like a seal over your heart, like a seal on your arm. For love is as strong as death, jealousy is as severe as Sheol; **its flashes are flashes of fire**, **the very flame of the LORD**.

I felt strongly that I needed to search this out. No matter how long it took, it seemed absolutely crucial that I understand this scripture. So I labored over it for a few weeks...months. Nothing came to me. No real insight came, no wisdom grew. I felt so stupid! It seemed to me that other people really 'got' this and I wondered if I ever would.

A few days later, my husband and I went to a small prayer meeting. There was just a hand-full of people there. One guy sitting next to me all of a sudden said, "My hands are burning up! Who needs prayer?" Before I could say anything, he grabbed my hands and started praying. Immediately I saw a vision. In this vision I was a horse. I was standing in a place that was completely black. There was nothing to see in any direction except a burning trail of fire. The flames were white, yellow, red, orange and blue, as though it was a gas/oil fire. I was walking in the middle of the flame as the Lord led me. His hand was in my mouth instead of a bit. The Lord looked forward, so I looked forward and there was no end to the darkness illuminated only by the fiery path. Then He looked behind us, so I looked behind us and there was again no end to the lighted path in that direction either. Then I saw Him smile. The vision was over.

I started to cry and the man who was holding my hands praying for me asked me what I saw. I asked him how he knew that I saw anything. He just smiled and asked again. I described the vision and kept on crying. He asked me what I thought it meant. I said it probably meant that my life had been difficult and that it would probably continue to be difficult for the rest of my life. (I was a little discouraged…can you tell?) He laughed and said, "No, that's not what your vision means." Then he opened his Bible and started to read the Song of Solomon, Chapter 8. He said something like: "The Lord is showing you that His passion for His bride has no beginning and has no end. It will never fade or go out because it is lit with the oil of the Holy Spirit. All others things are meaningless compared to His love for us…that's why everything was black around you. He led you with His hand in your mouth because He wants you to stop questioning His passion for you and the passion He will give you for Him. He leads you. Go with Him!"

Then I started to cry again. The Lord had answered my hearts cry to know His passion. He showed me then that the blackest black of circumstances could not put out His passion for me and you. It is as strong as death and as unyielding as the grave. **This fiery passion will not be vanquished**.

I have been told that I was a horse in that vision because horses are a sign of human strength. I do have a tendency to lean on my own strength, so that is probably true. But with this vision the Lord was calling me to a deeper understanding.

1 Cor 2:10
For to us God revealed them through the Spirit; for **the Spirit searches all things, even the <u>depths of God</u>.**

He is inviting me to go with Him…to allow Him to lead me into depths I had not considered…TO TRULY **KNOW** THE PASSION OF HIS HEART! I no longer have to settle for someone else's words of wisdom or insight. I suppose we have never had to rely on other people to see Him for ourselves since we can always receive from Him, but I wasn't aware or awake enough to His passion to go and see Him for myself.

I am reminded of a scripture that I think reveals some of God's heart about passion.

Rom 9:13
Just as it is written, "Jacob I loved, but Esau I hated."

We all know that Jacob was a bit of a scoundrel. He lied, deceiving his own dad to get what was rightfully his brother's. But his brother, Esau, threw it away for momentary satisfaction. Jacob valued the blessing of God given through his earthly father enough to do anything to get it. Esau didn't care. He just threw it away. Now, I'm not saying that Jacob was perfect, but how can we ignore what God says about him. The Lord loved the passion that Jacob had for Him and all He had to give. And God blessed him for it!

In the 90's, when Wade and I were a part of the leadership of our previous church, we both received a 'word' from our pastor. The following was what the Lord gave to me through our pastor.

Gayle, you are a spiritual lobbyist with a passion to confront the issues that others would rather leave alone. You are bold, tenacious and zealous toward the things of God. You have a prophetic anointing with a desire to intercede to bring forth the will of God in any given situation. You are loyal in your relationships to people. You have great compassion for those who are hurting and abused. You are a spiritual activist who wrestles with God. Your giftedness is necessary to displace complacency and lethargy in the body.

Personally, I relate most easily to a wrestling 'Jacob' spirit than to a apathetic 'Esau' spirit.

The Lord causes me to want more. He enlarges my spirit to hear His questions to my heart. I'll be reading His word and He'll ask, 'What am I saying to YOU in this scripture?' That or some other seemingly little question will start a lesson of a lifetime. A whole pile of keys is found when He uses one key to unlock a door.

Do I have a complete understanding of passion? No, and I hope that I never stop trying to plumb the **depths of God** on this subject or any other.

The scripture in the Song of Solomon that says love is as strong as death intrigues me. His love and passion for us took Him to His death. His passion waits for the world to embrace His love and LIVE free of the second death! I must KNOW this passion!

## THE KEY OF REST

Rest is an elusive thing in our culture. Many of us tend to be workaholics, ever striving for the means to do and have what we want with less and less time to enjoy it. I am one of the many women in our society that struggles frequently with insomnia. So we are apt to work like dogs while lacking sleep which can make us a cranky, disagreeable lot. And God forbid we should be premenstrual at the same time. What a nightmare that is for the men in our lives!

When I was in high school and going through puberty, my mom was going through menopause. My dad used to walk through the kitchen and if we were bickering he'd say, "Dive, dive. INCOMING!!! Move to safer depths!" Then he would hide out in his office until the coast was clear. We were both cranky and far too tired to think straight. We needed rest.

Heb 3:18-19
18 And to whom did He swear that they should not enter His rest, but to those who were disobedient?
19 And so **we see that they were not able to enter because of unbelief.**

In the above scripture we see that unbelief was the sin that kept the Israelites from entering into God's rest. He considered their unbelief a road block to receiving His provision, which we know is Jesus Christ. They refused the Lord's gift of peace and rest through Jesus, and were striving to enter in their own way, which is impossible. They rejected His provision, just as we do when we willingly enter into unbelief.

In the early 90's, I did some lobbying. I worked for pro-family, politically conservative organizations. To say that I loved it would be GREATLY understating how I felt about that job. All day, every day it consumed my thoughts, and though I claimed to be doing it for the glory of God, when I look back I can see that was not true. I cared about it too much. I elevated it above my family and even above God. My passion for politics far outweighed my devotion to anything else. As I remember those days, I have a hard time believing that I was ever like that. I was single focused on the wrong thing and everybody around me suffered for it.

Striving and driven were two words that described me well: ever pressing, urging and passionate about 'the cause'. I must have driven everyone around me crazy. I had no peace or rest in my life, weighted down with all the cares of the world…trusting the people that I worked with and myself to 'make something happen'.

One day I was going someplace with my boss and he said something about my 'always striving' for something and as the week progressed, several people commented on how much I was always striving. I didn't realize it but I must have been doing it a lot if people were seeing it and telling me.

Since I recognized that striving was not good…I started to strive to stop striving! As I'm sure that you can guess, that didn't work. In fact, my striving not to strive increased my striving. Round and round I went, hopelessly spinning.

That's when I started getting very sick. It got bad enough that after a while I had to quit work. I was very angry with God. I felt that He had stripped me of what I loved. I was completely blind to what the Lord was trying to do in me. I simply wanted what I wanted when I wanted it. Like a spoiled child, I begged for my own way. But the Lord in His wisdom said 'No'.

Finally I yielded to the Lord. I stopped fighting against Him and His voice. I let Him talk to me …and I began to listen again. I found a comfort I didn't realize I had lost. I needed to find myself…my worth within Him. I had been guilty of trying to find my value outside of Him, and that was a never – ending job. What real worth do we possess separate from Him?

There is peace inside of Him. It is quiet and calm. The warmth of His love changed my mind without me noticing. And it was easy because I didn't have to DO anything. I could just BE with Him and He changed my mind. I think that I had spent too much time and effort making things harder than they really were.

Matt 11:30
"For My yoke is easy, and My load is light."

A yoke is meant to restrain us and a load is meant to be carried. But I abandoned His yoke and load for my own creation. By taking my own yoke instead of yielding to Him, I sacrificed the peace that only comes from relinquishing my plans for His.

One day, a few years later, I was counseling someone about trusting the Lord. The person looked at me and asked how I could have the rest that I had. How did I get it? That woman did not know the 'me' of a few years before. I said that I didn't know how I got it because I used to have a terrible time with striving. I promised to pray and ask the Lord how He made that happen.

The Lord showed me as I spent time with Him and learned again to value Him and His word first, He packed it for me. It was as though I was on a trip. And when I arrived, I found that I had more in my suitcase than I realized. He put the peace and the rest inside of me when I wasn't paying attention. I had it when I needed it because He packed it for me. It's like the fringe benefits that come with your paycheck. You don't pay for them….(health insurance, vacation…) your employer does. God's a great boss!

Now I find it ironic that at this very moment I am wrestling with the Lord about this very issue again. The Sabbath rest of God is once again beyond my comprehension. I have just come through a battle of faith, which cost me all that I am. The Lord in His sovereignty chose to answer 'No' again to my request.

Intellectually, I realize that I have been purchased by His blood and I am not my own anymore. I choose to be His servant, so whatever He wants to do in my life needs to be fine with me...but I must confess that emotionally, I am wrestling and looking for the God of Peace that will soon crush Satan under my feet.

Heb 3:18, 19  And to whom did He swear that they would not enter His rest, but **to those who were (CHOSE TO BE) disobedient**?

And so we see that **they were not ABLE to enter because of unbelief**.

In the scripture above we see that first they **chose not** to enter into His rest. But then we see that in Hebrews 3:19 they were **unable** to enter in because of unbelief.

I say honestly that I believe He is good and He has my best interests at heart. But also honestly, my heart is somehow still sometimes disconnected with the 'feeling' of that truth. I am unsatisfied with a purely intellectual assent to belief. I want my faith to be wrapped up in passion and cushioned in peace.

God is so patient with me. Maybe in a few years, I will once again be able to measure the rest that He is packing for me even now. My bags are packed and I am traveling...but when I get to where He is leading me...I suspect that I will again find more treasures that He has 'secretly' packed for me. The testimony I choose in the 'in between time' is that He is good!

## THE KEY OF LETTING YOUR HEART TAKE COURAGE - HOPE

Heb 6:19
This **hope we have as an anchor of the soul**, a hope both sure and steadfast and one which enters within the veil

Hope is an anchor. It keeps me in line with the dreams that God has for me and those for which I pray. He makes me anticipate with great expectation what He will bring about because He has planted hope in my heart. He lifts my vision higher with that miracle believing hope.

My husband and I have two children. Our daughter's name is Maranda, and our son's name is Jered. When our daughter was six years old, I received a prophetic word. It was a long detailed word regarding our past, present and our future. It touched each family member. But the part of the word that really got my attention at that time was a specific word about Maranda. It referred to her future marriage. I took notice of that because Maranda was scheduled for open-heart surgery within the next month. She has a congenital heart block that requires her to have a pacemaker. This open-heart surgery was to repair a hole in her heart. There were obvious risks and we were uncertain as to her survival. When I heard that part of the 'word', I was filled with hope. She will be fine, I thought. We had so much peace during the surgery that we actually fell asleep in the waiting room. The nurse commented to us that parents never fall asleep while waiting during a procedure like open-heart surgery. We told her that we had been assured by God that she had a set future…so it was easy to trust Him for her life.

Ps 27:13-14
13 I would have despaired **unless I had believed** that I would see the goodness of the LORD in the land of the living.
14 Wait for the LORD; be strong, and **LET your heart take courage**; yes, wait for the LORD.

I had been given the above scripture when Maranda was a baby. It has always reminded me to LET my heart take hold of the courage in His word. It has been a lifeline in troubled times.

About eighteen years later, I was in intensive care at the hospital. I apparently was not responding well. Basically, I was on my way out. And you know what? I was fine with that…I had given up. I was tired of fighting a disease that wouldn't leave me alone, as it seemed to me that I had suffered enough.

By way of background: I was diagnosed with Lupus and as mentioned earlier, had struggled with it for most of my life. This is the cause of Maranda's heart problems. This particular hospital visit was because the lupus had literally strangled my gall bladder. I didn't have any gallstones…but when lupus attacks an organ it tries to choke it to death. They had taken it out through laser surgery, but I had 'phantom' pain. So they thought that they had perforated the bowel…so they did the whole surgery over again and cut me stem to stern! Anyway, I wasn't recovering…so back to the story above…

I remember lying there, drugged up with morphine. My daughter came in and bent down to my ear and whispered, "I'M NOT MARRIED YET… YOU HAVE TO BE THERE! YOUR PRESENCE AT MY WEDDING IS A PART OF THE WORD. FIGHT!!!"

When she said that, it was as though I was awakened from a dream. From that moment I began to recover. I had lost my faith and my vision…I was hopeless. Maranda reminded me of the hope I have in His word. He is true to His word! Incidentally, Maranda's middle name is Hope!

Num 23:19
"**God is not a man, that He should lie**, nor a son of man, that He should repent; has He said, and will He not do it? Or has He spoken, and will He not make it good?

There are many words that the Lord has given me that have yet to come to pass. And the enemy is ever trying to rob me of my hope in Him. But I remember His faithfulness and I CHOOSE to trust His word! I hope in Him that He WILL make it good!

## ONE TRIAL – FOUR KEYS

Several years ago, I was dealing with a peculiar aspect of lupus. I was in a period of about eight days of little or no sleep. It wasn't simply insomnia. A painful rash covered my body from head to toe. During this time, I was able to collect four keys.

## THE KEY OF FREEDOM FROM SELF PITY

One night as I sat in our living room, trying not to scratch my skin off from all of the itching, I realized I was consumed with self-pity. But the worst part about that was I felt justified. God was choosing not to rescue me…so I didn't need to have the 'right' attitude of faith…He had abandoned me. And since He didn't appear to care about me…I didn't care about pleasing Him! I'm sure you are noticing a pattern in my life…I'm a whiner. My mom says that I don't whine to other people…but in my soul…I am a whiner! OK…now that I have admitted what I am sure you already figured out…we can continue…

About three days into this trial, the Lord gave me a vision. I saw a seal swimming and playing in a big pool. The seal was jumping up out of the water, balancing a beach ball on his nose and jumping through colorful hoops suspended above the water.

Then the picture expanded. As the picture got wider, I realized that the seal was not in a pool but was swimming in a large drum of black oil. I was alarmed because I couldn't imagine how he could possibly survive that?

At that moment, I heard the **Lord say to me, "You are the seal. The black oil is self-pity. And you are not merely swimming in it but frolicking."**

Self-pity is like quicksand to the soul. Before you know it you're knee deep and sinking faster every minute. The only truly effective rope of deliverance that can aid our escape is contrite repentance.

Our self-pity causes us to elevate our circumstances above the provision of God. It is putting ourselves and how we feel first. When we are filled with it we seem to be asking the world around us to take notice of our pitiful situation and give us attention and sympathy. It is faithlessness in God's ability to bring us through to a better understanding of His love and perfect timing. And with that new understanding, deliverance may still elude us. But if we can catch a glimpse of His cross and the fact that He went through it 'for the Joy' that was coming…Wow what a revelation! Truly a key to freedom!

Immediately I saw how I was choosing to sin against God by frolicking in self-pity and how offensive that sin was to Him. He led me through repentance that night. And every time I am tempted to indulge in self-pity, He is faithful to remind me of the sin He was gracious enough to free me from. We get to choose…I choose again and again to remember that He loves me no matter what circumstances say.

Rom 2:4
Or do you think lightly of the riches of His kindness and forbearance and patience, not knowing that **the kindness of God leads you to <u>repentance</u>**?

Several years ago, Wade and I participated in a home meeting. All of us were committed to be very open and real with each other. There was a man in the group that was coming out of the homosexual lifestyle. His father had not paid much attention to him growing up and he felt neglected. An inadequacy grew inside of him, and he medicated himself with unhealthy relationships. He was and is wounded. But this wound became the reason or excuse to remain immature.

After years of listening to his lament, I couldn't stand it any more. I looked at him and asked, "How old are you?" His reply was that he was forty years old. "How old will you be before you decide to be a man? Nobody had a perfect earthly dad. Some of the people in this very room have dealt with extreme abuse, as well as neglect. When will you choose to rise above your painful memories and be the man that God has called you to be?"

I'm sure I could have said it with more kindness, and in a more private setting, but I do care about him. Even now, whenever I think of him or go by his house, I pray for him. I pray that he will choose to forgive his father completely and by doing so, find freedom for himself.

<u>We get to choose</u>. We can use our past as an excuse not to grow. Or we can use it as a diving board. We can learn to do flips and spins and even leap off the high dive of freedom and liberty found in the true and passionate nature of God. Or we can limit ourselves, imposing pitiful constraints upon our own hearts.

You may be reading this right now thinking…"What does she know about suffering?" And "How can she know how discouraged I am?" Let me just be real here for a moment and tell you that I know what it's like to be seduced by the enemy. Suicide is a very seductive lure. It seems so easy when life feels like one long exercise in endurance. I'm not trying to step all over your feelings or mine for that matter. Go ahead and be real… 'Feel' it. But for your sake and everyone around you, don't pitch a tent inside of the breach you are experiencing right now. Because then the enemy wins twice. He gets to ruin and torment you and then blind you to the hope that is real…because God is real…even if you can't 'feel' His presence at this very moment.

Job 23 says it best:

8 "Behold, I go forward but He is not *there,*
And backward, but I cannot perceive Him;
9 When He acts on the left, I cannot behold *Him;*
He turns on the right, I cannot see Him.
10 "But He knows the way I take;
*When* He has tried me, I shall come forth as gold.
11 "My foot has held fast to His path;
I have kept His way and not turned aside.
12 "I have not departed from the command of His lips;
I have treasured the words of His mouth more
than my necessary food.
13 "But He is unique and who can turn Him?
And *what* His soul desires, that He does.
14 "For He performs what is appointed for me,
And many such *decrees* are with Him.
15 "Therefore, I would be dismayed at His presence;
*When* I consider, I am terrified of Him.
16 "*It is* God *who* has made my heart faint,
And the Almighty *who* has dismayed me,
17 But I am not silenced by the darkness,
Nor deep gloom *which* covers me.

Freedom beckons in His timing…repentance is our 'Get Out Of Jail FREE' card. But **we** have to choose freedom. We won't live long in the black oil of self pity.

Vs.14 on talks about how more difficulties may come our way. We may suffer fear and our hearts may faint. But we can't let the darkness silence us. The Truth is still the Truth. He is real. **HE is the living, breathing, walking, and talking TRUTH.** And we are His. We signed up to be His and to trust Him to love us and know what we need…and want. We can choose to rely on Him no matter what because the truth is, He is good.

## THE KEY OF REPAIRING THE BREACH

A couple of days later, I was given an open vision. For those of you who have not experienced it, an open vision is just like being there. I was in my living room, but I was actually in the vision. I wasn't just seeing it in my mind's eye. It was as though I was actually there in the vision. It's hard to explain, but it was sort of like in a dream when you are actually experiencing the dream…but I wasn't asleep.

Back to the vision…The Lord led me by the hand out to a desert. It wasn't a desert like the Sahara; it was more like the desert in a cowboy movie with tumbleweeds and those trees that look kind of scruffy and half dead. He put His arm around me and was pointing to a distant patch of land. That far off place was green with lots of beautiful green trees and a great variety of healthy, lush plants. I knew it was a long way off because it looked so small from where we were standing. The only words He said to me were, "I will lead you there."

Then I was back in my living room by myself again, sitting in my chair. This seemed so weird/real to me that I got up and went into the bathroom to wash my face and try to shake it off. When I grabbed the towel, I looked into the mirror and saw Him again (by saying that I saw Him…I mean I saw someone my spirit recognized as God). He said, "This journey will take you through many broken places…many breaches. I will repair them. I will let you come with Me as I repair them. But first you must let Me repair the breaches here." And as He said that, He pointed to my heart.

I realized He was saying that my broken places needed to be mended. The journey to my own healing would be long and time consuming. But, if I would let Him, He would repair the breaches inside of me. He gave me a promise that I could go with Him as He was repairing other breaches in His body…His church…His family…if I would allow Him to start with me. Again, He was giving me a choice.

Isa 58:12
"And those from among you will rebuild the ancient ruins; you will raise up the age-old foundations; and you will be called the **repairer of the breach**, the restorer of the streets in which to dwell.

A breach is a chasm in a relationship; an opening created by a misunderstanding, a disagreement or a wound that has not yet been healed. We are all living stones connecting with other 'stones' to form the house of God. Sometimes the mortar between can get damaged from neglect. A breach must not be allowed to remain, because if we don't make the necessary repairs the wall will become unstable and eventually, when left unattended, it will crumble. If relationships are not healed, the wound comes again and again in other associations. If we settle for moving on to the next friendship without the healing, the wisdom that comes from working through the problem is lost.

Individuals that allow breaches to remain are often immature and even prone to cause breaches wherever they go. This *'problem'* doesn't follow them…it lives inside of them. We must learn to turn away from this pattern of wounding and being wounded. We must choose to stop running and deal with the rifts we have with one another. This requires great courage, because dealing with the problem starts with looking in the mirror. There is usually something to be repented of before you go to the other person with the *'sliver extractor'*!

In order to repair the breaches we must first go to the breach. Seems obvious, doesn't it? But, many of us want the healing without actually going to the breach (the problem, the wound, or the disagreement).

We have to be willing to try to understand how the other person feels. The kindness of the Lord leads all of us to repentance. But we can only live His kindness if we put ourselves in the wounded person's shoes. And how can we do that if we won't hear them and try to understand.

The next difficulty that often comes is when people are willing to go to the place of wounding, but then choose to live there. Living inside the breach is an easy way to get sympathy. The people who choose to pitch a tent inside the breach state the reasons for their wounds with such conviction we can get drawn into the drama. This so called 'mercy' is cruel and is selfish. This 'mercy' seeks to be thought of as 'kind and caring' but in truth is extremely unloving. We do them a disservice by this false love masquerading as mercy making them comfortable in the jail cell they have created for themselves inside the wound. Letting them stay in a hurtful place and look at it, talk about it and let the wound fester, instead of allowing God to use us to bring them through the process to freedom is lazy at best. Our freedom from bitterness, unforgiveness and even hatred has already been purchased. If we choose bondage, or we let a friend feel comfortable with that choice, how disappointed the Lord must be. Jesus died for our freedom! There are no victims in His family…only the redeemed! We need to take hold of the keys of repentance and forgiveness and unlock the jail cell.

Eph 4:13
until we all attain to the unity of the faith, and of the knowledge of the Son of God, **to a mature man, to the measure of the stature which belongs to the fullness of Christ.**

We can choose to forgive and grow up into Him…which is true freedom… the ultimate repair. If we allow the Lord to heal us and our relationships with each other, we can be rightly fitted into the wall with strong and healthy connections. Living stones, joined with grace. We are all called to be the "repairers of the breaches"!

## **THE KEY OF MOMENTARY LIGHT AFFLICTION**

2 Cor 4:16-18
16 Therefore we do not lose heart, but though our outer man is decaying, yet our inner man is being renewed day by day.
17 For **momentary, light affliction** is producing for us an **eternal weight of glory** far beyond all comparison,
18 while we look not at the things which are seen, but at the things which are not seen; for the things which are seen are temporal, but the things which are not seen are eternal.

Suffering is a funny thing. It's very subjective. But for most people, their own suffering seems worse than anybody else's. If you ask some of my closest friends, they would probably say that I had suffered physically a lot. And when I'm in it, it feels pretty bad.

My husband once referred to our struggle together (with my health challenges) as being like a prisoner of war. They are captured and treated with extreme cruelty. This brutality is demoralizing and is meant to break people down and rob them of themselves as well as their very hope. Without hope, life can feel like an exercise in endurance.

But honestly, I can look around me at any point and see someone dealing with things that are much more difficult. I have my vision, hearing and most of the time I am able to walk and function fine. Living in the United States also affords me the opportunity to access the medical services I need. In fact, a lot of people don't even know that I have lupus!

However, I must confess that when I'm at a point of indescribable pain…. it doesn't feel momentary or light! That's when I need to remind myself of what He endured for the **joy** set before Him. The hope of heaven keeps me going sometimes. I let my imagination take me there because I know that whatever I can visualize is far less than what it will really be like.

Pain can also be exhausting. And I'm not just talking about the drowsiness of the pain meds. The amount of energy it takes to just appear normal seems like too much sometimes. So I get cranky and short tempered. I usually don't want to tell people why I'm being so short with them…I don't want them to see me as 'the person with a disease'.

I was raised in the Catholic Church. Each time I would enter and see the statue of Jesus hanging on the cross, awe would come over me. As a child I often thought, "Wow! He must really love me, because I sure wouldn't go through all that for anybody."

I have previously mentioned the "Cross of Christ Proves He is Good" plaque hanging in my living room. And sometimes I reconsider His last day as a man here on earth when I am feeling low and disappointed with my life. He'd hang out with His best friends, have dinner, and watch one of His buddies sell Him out. Later, knowing the pain and humiliation that was coming, He asked His Dad for courage and strength to give up His life for people who had no idea of the magnitude of His gift. He must have thought that it was going to be the worst day of His life…and one of the most important. I really can't wrap my mind around the weight of His emotions in the garden as He literally sweat blood

I have yet to comprehend the 'eternal weight of glory' mentioned in the previous verse. **But** - for the JOY set before us, we would surely give in to discouragement and faithlessness. Now when I consider what He suffered…I can't help but remember HOW He suffered. He did it with joy. This is my most noble ambition.

How can I weigh my 'momentary light affliction' against His weighty glory? It seems silly to place them on the same eternal scale.

## THE KEY OF TEARING DOWN AND REBUILDING

Prov 15:25
The **LORD will <u>tear down</u> the house of the proud**, but He will establish the boundary of the widow.

Jer 1:10
"See, I have appointed you this day over the nations and over the kingdoms, to pluck up and to **break down**, to destroy and to overthrow, **to build** and to plant."

Near the end of the 'sleepless time', I had another vision. It was a cartoon. I know, it sounds weird. I thought it was weird too! Anyway, here it is: A little man who looked like one of the Mario Brothers from the video game stood in sparkling white overalls. He had a white wheelbarrow full of perfect white bricks (they seemed to resemble rectangular pearls) and a container of mortar that looked like it was made of glitter. One by one he would take a brick out of the barrel, put mortar on it and set it in place, then stand back and admire his work. Sometimes, as he got some of the glitter on the face of the white pearl bricks, he would wipe it off with his white handkerchief. After a while, I'm not sure how long, he stood back, rubbed his hands together and then bowed to me, as if the say, "Didn't I do a fabulous job? Isn't it perfect?"

My only thought was, 'This is so weird'. I didn't hear the Lord but I sensed His presence. I felt He wanted me to know that I had built a near perfect wall around myself. I had put a lot of effort into it and was very proud of my accomplishment. I could keep people distant while having the appearance of godliness, when my greatest motive was to protect myself.

I felt as though He was looking right through me.

Before I can describe the wall and how it was built, I need to explain why I thought I needed the wall in the first place. In general, I am a fairly confident person. I know who the Lord has called me to be and I am making my way down that road to His destination. But I have a few insecurities as well. The reason that I constructed this wall is because I felt vulnerable to people who were suffering from seemingly greater insecurities than mine.

Let me stop here and confess a significant belief I have. In my opinion, extremely insecure people can be some of the most dangerous people on the planet. Their target is almost always those that appear to be more secure than them selves. They seem to want to make presumably strong people deficient in some way so that they can feel better or validated in them selves. And people whom they suppose are stronger than they are can't respond by confronting the situation; because we are stronger so they should be able to take it. I have inadvertently helped these poor little insecure people to make this error of not realizing how much damage they are doing by hiding behind my carefully constructed wall of 'confidence'.

This wall of protection that I referred to took on two different appearances. The first way that I raised the wall was to intimidate these people into not talking to me at all. You probably already know, but just in case you don't, I'll tell you; to the degree that you can speak life into someone's heart…with that same degree of power you can speak death. Sometimes I think I know what I can say to lift someone out of the pit…and by the same token, I sometimes know how I can send them there. It used to be hard for me to resist when threatened. It's like a phrase that I heard once, 'Real power is knowing you can…but you don't!' I used to hope eventually I wouldn't hear the enemy's voice of cruelty. But now I realize whether I hear him or not, I must always choose to love, not hate.

The second appearance of the wall was to look unscathed. I would show no sign of injury, pretending that what was said didn't matter, or I often simply laughed it off. In short, I lied. I was not honest about how I felt. So in my deception and cowardice, I increased their lack of understanding and built my wall higher. The foundation of the wall was made of lies.

The Lord let me know it was time to take it all down. Fear rose up in me. I was afraid that He would take a wrecking ball and knock it down all at once. But then I saw the little man again with his ladder taking down one brick at a time, wiping them off as he went and neatly stacking them into the barrel again. I thought, 'This is going to take forever!' But then I sensed the Lord's whisper, "It will take as long as you need."

I was being asked by the Lord to learn a new way; to expose myself and be honest. He wanted me to let my guard down and risk additional pain. Initially, it was a terrifying prospect. I imagined it might have been something like Superman walking up to the lead box but the Kryptonite was not inside the box…it was sitting on top. The analogy isn't perfect because being real or honest won't literally kill me the way Kryptonite kills Superman...It is, however, a dying to self in order to be more like Jesus.

He is my only refuge. I must choose to let Him be my refuge! By taking apart the wall slowly, He has taught me that I really CAN trust Him. His more perfect way is best for me. A hedge of protection by the power of the Holy Spirit and Love is all I need to be safe.

Jer 17:7
"Blessed is the man who trusts in the LORD and **whose <u>trust</u> is the LORD.**

The Lord revealed the place or the 'walls' where He likes to meet with me. I call it the furnace room. I'll describe the view from my mind's eye. The room is made of metal. Everything in the room is metal as well. The floor, walls and furniture are made of various colors and types of metal. There is no ceiling in this room. Everything in and of the room is transparent and when I go inside, I am see-through too. Through the walls and through the furniture you can see the yellow, orange, red and the hints of blue in the flames that surround the room. Everything is warm, not hot. All of it is soft to the touch. As I walk on the floor, my feet seem to sink into it as if it were made of the foam on a really comfortable mattress. When I lay down on the couch, I sink into it as if it were a feather bed. And I feel warm and secure.

In this room no secret can be kept because everything is transparent. Every thought, motive, hope, sorrow and dream is exposed. I have often been grateful that there is no ceiling because it feels like there is no limit to His love for me in the furnace room.

I experience His love but at the same time I feel a holy fear when I enter. He always knows me fully, but in that place of heat, I am aware that the only truly Consuming Fire surrounds me. My sin is laid bare and repentance is a lifestyle within the furnace room as well as when I am outside of it, I hope! I would like to write that I go there often and stay as long as I can. But honestly, it's easier to remember the fear of the Lord than His love sometimes. My flesh resists until I once again hear His call to enter in. It costs me greatly to enter His place of exposure. It is not ever easy to enter into His heart. Like the eye of the needle, when entering one must remove all hindrances to passage. I must choose to be raw, naked and completely bare before Him. Transparency is the choice I must make before I cross the threshold.

In the furnace room and <u>in life itself the walls **He** constructs for me are crystal clear</u>. I can't hide from Him. I can only hide inside of Him and become an untainted Christian. My hope is some day you will look at me and see Him looking through.

Isa 49:16
"Behold, I have inscribed you on the palms of My hands; **your <u>walls</u> are continually before me**.

In this verse the walls are described in the Strong's Concordance as being walls of protection. He protects us within Himself…He is our wall of protection.

So now we can either choose to build our own walls to hide behind, or allow the Lord to build the room best suited to us. All of these keys offer us a choice. The only way that a key works is to turn it when inserted in the proper hole. Each key is unique and fits only one hole inside of us; one way of living. Will we choose to open the door and be transparent or keep it shut tight and locked? It's scary to let Him help you take down your walls…I know…but He is gentle…And it will take as long as you need too!

## **THE KEY OF THE WORD BEING A LADDER**

One Sunday, as I sat on the same pew that I always sat on, I had a strange experience. It was before the service and my husband was in our pastor's office praying with the other elders of the church. My head was bowed as I pretended to pray. What I was really doing was complaining to God. I was really mad at Him. Things were not going well for me, even though to the casual observer, I probably looked fine. But my heart was not right, and my disappointment was turning to bitterness. While I was silently yelling at God, He gave me a vision. It was as follows: I was walking through a forest at mid-day. The sun was bright and warm but the shade from the trees provided some relief from the heat and the glare. Suddenly, I tripped and began sliding down a steep crevasse. No matter what I did, I could not stop the slide. Deeper and deeper I slid until day seemed to turn to night. I felt something around my ankle pulling me deeper still. It was some sort of vine. Frightened, I cried out the only thing that came to my mind. Your word is a light to my path… "I NEED A LIGHT!" Instantly the Lord said, "Look up." So I did. A few pews in front of me sat a man. He was wearing 501 Levi jeans and a flannel shirt. This man had long hair, a bushy mustache and I think he had a beard. When I looked at him the Lord told me that he had my light.

At this point in my life, I was so politically conservative I squeaked when I walked. I was quite the Pharisee. I judged him the moment that I saw him and decided I didn't need anything he had to give. So I told God to tell someone else the word because there was no way that I was going to talk to that man.

The Lord did not respond. My disobedience was met with the kind of silence that is deafening. I begged the Lord to please just tell me Himself. SILENCE! After waiting quite a while, I realized God was not going to give me what I wanted in the way that I wanted it. So, knowing that my need was great, I got up and walked over to the man and said, "Move over, I have to talk to you". He just looked at me like I was crazy. "Didn't you hear me? I have to talk to you. MOVE OVER!" The poor guy was stunned at my rudeness but he moved over and I introduced myself and told him my story. When I was finished telling him the vision I asked him for 'my light'. He said that he was sorry but he didn't have a 'light' for me. I assured him he did, but he just didn't know that he did. I told him it was probably whatever he had been reading or studying lately. Once again he apologized and said he didn't have a word for me, but he would be willing to pray for me. When I consider that exchange now, he was very brave to offer. I however, said 'NO thanks' and went back to my seat even angrier with the Lord.

The next week was not a pleasant week for my family. I was pretty hard to live with during that time. The following Sunday I sat in my same seat and I felt a tap on my shoulder. There he was with a grin on his face. "I have that 'light' for you now if you still need it!" he happily said. "Well, good, 'cause I need it even more now!" was my reply.

Zeph 3:12-20
12 "But I will leave among you a humble and lowly people, and they will take refuge in the name of the LORD.
13 "The remnant of Israel will do no wrong and tell no lies, nor will a deceitful tongue be found in their mouths; for they shall feed and lie down with no one to make them tremble."
14 Shout for joy, O daughter of Zion! Shout in triumph, O Israel! Rejoice and exult with all your heart, O daughter of Jerusalem!
15 The LORD has taken away His judgments against you, He has cleared away your enemies. The King of Israel, the LORD, is in your midst; **you will fear disaster no more**.
16 In that day it will be said to Jerusalem: "**Do not be afraid, O Zion; do not let your hands fall limp**. (Discouragement)
17 "The LORD your God is in your midst, a victorious warrior. He will exult over you with joy, He will be quiet in His love, He will rejoice over you with shouts of joy. (HE WILL DANCE)
18 "I will gather those who grieve about the appointed feasts-- they came from you, O Zion; the reproach of exile is a burden on them.
19 "Behold, I am going to deal at that time with all your oppressors, I will save the lame and gather the outcast, and I will turn their shame into praise and renown in all the earth.
20 "At that time I will bring you in, even at the time when I gather you together; indeed, I will give you renown and praise among all the peoples of the earth, **when I restore your fortunes before your eyes**," says the LORD.

He began to read the above verses. As I listened, two things were happening to me. The first was that my mind was telling me it didn't make sense and that this scripture had nothing to do with my life. Secondly, I began to sob. I almost couldn't control my crying and I didn't even know why. The thing that alarmed me the most was that up to that point I never cried in front of people. If I was sad about something I used to get up in the middle of the night when everybody in the house was asleep and cry alone. I mentioned earlier in this book when I was pregnant with our daughter, we were unsure about her survival. For those last three months of pregnancy I walked on eggshells wondering if I would still be pregnant the next day. I pretended to be 'fine' (the Christian F word). I would pretend to be full of faith in front of the world, go to bed at night, and lay there until Wade was asleep, then get up and cry for an hour or two. I was too prideful to let anyone see me at a 'weak' moment, even my own husband.

(Back to the story) He finished reading the scripture; my heart was broken and I couldn't hide it. So he began to pray for me. I knew no peace. My head and my heart were at war, but somehow I knew this word was the key. God had given me this 'light' and I had to use it.

Every morning for the next thirty-one days I woke up to it. I read it, meditated on it and prayed it. Read it again and again. One morning about fifteen days into this process I had another little vision. I saw myself climbing a rope ladder out of that crevasse I had fallen into. I realized each time I embraced this 'light', this scripture; the Lord was providing it as my way of escape. I didn't know how long it would take; I just knew that I needed to stick with it until I was free from that blinding darkness. On the thirty first day I was free. I can't explain it; I just had a new heart somehow. God did a miracle in me and I am forever grateful!

Now when I am in a place of discouragement or even despair, I search the Word for His 'word' or 'light' to me and use it as a ladder to climb out and be free. His word is the light that we need when hope is darkened.

I have been careful not to name too many names in this book, but I have to tell you the name of this man with the 'light'. His name is Troy, and he has encouraged me a lot in my walk with the Lord. It's hard to believe after such a rocky start, but Troy and I are good friends.

I found out years later that I had been praying for him before we even met. Our pastor had asked us to pray for one of his friends to come back to the Lord. That request came to us at least 5 years before I ever met Troy…

but he was my pastor's friend. I guess the Lord knew that I would need that 'light'! The Lord let me be a part of His provision for me…God's so smart, isn't He!

## THE KEY OF REPENTING OF BLINDNESS

I've only had one best friend in my life besides my husband. We talked almost every day, even more than that sometimes. I held nothing back from her, trusting her completely. I thought I knew her as well as she knew me. Eventually, I realized I didn't really know her at all.

I was so happy in this friendship that I chose not to see anything that might hinder it. But there were things happening that were odd and beyond justification. I would explain it away in my heart by saying something like, 'Oh, that's just how she and her husband are.'

But there was corruption happening in that house. It went farther than I could have ever imagined. If I told you what was happening you would be shocked. You might even wonder how I could have been so completely blind…as **I** often wonder to this very day.

Rev 3:15-19
15 'I know your deeds, that you are neither cold nor hot; I would that you were cold or hot.
16 'So because you are lukewarm, and neither hot nor cold, I will spit you out of My mouth.
17 'Because you say, "I am rich, and have become wealthy, and have need of nothing," and **you do not know that you are wretched and miserable and poor and <u>blind</u> and naked,**
18 I advise you to buy from Me gold refined by fire, that you may become rich, and white garments, that you may clothe yourself, and that the shame of your nakedness may not be revealed; and <u>**eye salve to anoint your eyes, that you may see**</u>.
19 'Those whom I love, I reprove and discipline; be **zealous therefore, and <u>repent</u>**.

I willingly believed a lie. I deluded myself into believing that everything was fine, ignoring the signs proving there were problems beneath the surface. <u>I needed the eye salve from the Lord in order to see the truth.</u>

Frankly, I loved myself more than them. I didn't want to see the truth; in fact, I ran from it. Their restoration to the Lord was not my main concern. I put my needs and desires above them. I didn't really love them because when you love someone the truth guides you. And at the time, the truth was inconvenient and I was selfish.

The Lord revealed the truth eventually. During that time, I was disciplined severely. It was the most costly trial and learning experience of my life. As part of the learning curve, the Lord gave me a dream. I think He did that because I refused to hear Him while I was awake so He graciously talked to me as I slept.

This was the dream:

I was in my house by myself in the middle of the day. I was tidying up. I saw our cat sitting on a living room chair sleeping. As I walked into the bedroom, I thought I saw the cat jumping onto a shelf and knocking everything off it. Liquid things in jars broke open and were piled in a mess of broken glass and liquid, as well as the other stuff that was on that shelf.

"Jazmin!" I yelled at our cat. But it wasn't Jazmin. It looked exactly like her, but it was a strange cat, an intruder in our home.

After cleaning up the mess, I went into the kitchen and caught the cat intruder messing up the kitchen. I finally realized I needed to get that cat out of our house. So I chased it all around until I caught it by the back of the neck. I picked it up and went to the door. While I held it, it clawed and scratched up my arm so much that my skin hung in ribbons and blood was pouring down my arm. I opened the door and literally threw the cat out into the street. Then I woke up.

My dreams tend to be kind of odd. I generally assume that they are of little consequence. But near the end of this nightmare trial, the Lord revealed the meaning to me and gave me the 1 Sam. scripture below. I had let strangers into my life and into my heart. They appeared to be familiar and safe. I didn't know them after the spirit. I knew them in my own blind flesh…and I was satisfied with that until **my** life was disrupted.

54

1 Sam 16:7
But the LORD said to Samuel, "Do not look at his appearance or at the height of his stature, because I have rejected him; for God sees not as man sees, for **man looks at the outward appearance, but the <u>LORD looks at the heart</u>.**"

I will always regret satisfying myself above other people who were wounded during that time. Other friends tried to help me see, but I lashed out at them. I hurt and alienated a lot of people. I even went to a police friend of mine, who was aware of the 'case', and begged him to believe the lie that I was hanging onto so tightly. He looked at me with the kind of expression that you might give to a homeless alcoholic as he tells you with slurred speech that his circumstances are the fault of others instead of himself.

I will probably never trust myself to truly KNOW anyone again.

Years later, I was misled by my desire for 'false' reality again. I wanted to believe someone so desperately that I chose again to be blind. I let my heart be manipulated and I made bad decisions because of it. Once again people were wounded because I was too afraid and selfish to see the truth.

This is the war inside of me: wanting to do and know TRUTH while at the same time wanting to be comfortable. **<u>Truth is often very uncomfortable and inconvenient</u>**! Most of the time, we would rather not address the truth of things because we mistakenly think that the absence of conflict is peace. But that isn't true! Peace is working through conflict to resolution. Sometimes we need to fight through problems. If we remain silent, pushing down what happened and not dealing with problems, then they build under the surface. It's like a pot being left on the stove. At first it is simmering but eventually the water will boil away. The pot burns and is often ruined. I am trying to learn to trust the Lord more with each trial as I see His faithfulness. And to allow Him to lead me out of willful blindness when/if I stumble again.

The pride of thinking that we KNOW is so dangerous. And we are not the only people wounded by this pride. We fall but so do others who trust our judgment. I have adopted a new rule of thumb for myself…I know I don't know…so I must trust Him to show me what and who is true or false. He sees the inside…all is transparent to Him…there is comfort in that.

## THE KEY OF DEATH FIRST THEN LIFE

Sometimes God will shake us to help us see what is weak and strong in our hearts. It's a reassessment time that is necessary for our souls.

Heb 12:26-27
26 And His voice shook the earth then, but now He has promised, saying," **Yet once more I will <u>shake</u> not only the earth, but also the heaven."**
27 And this expression "Yet once more," denotes the <u>removing of those things which can be shaken,</u> as of created things, <u>in order that those things which cannot be shaken may remain.</u>

<u>First, Death</u>:

The Lord showed me an old oak tree in a dream. It had a very thick trunk and branches that spread wide and tall. Though it was the end of fall, the tree still bore its brown, shriveled, dead leaves. I wondered how those leaves could have possibly remained.

Then within the dream the Lord spoke and said, "In My mercy, I will bring an earthquake."

Rom 11:22
**Behold then the <u>kindness and severity of God</u>**; to those who fell, severity, but to you, God's kindness, if you continue in His kindness; otherwise you also will be cut off.

The scripture above is pivotal in my life. I love this insight into God's soul. He is both kind and severe;
The beginning and the end…the Lamb of God and the Man of war. <u>He is severe mercy!</u> He will shake what is shakable so that what isn't remains steadfast and immovable.

The earthquake came. Many trees were damaged and uprooted. Cracks broke up the ground and the pavement. Broken glass from the windows of houses and cars littered the landscape. And many houses were moved off of their foundations.

Then I looked back at the oak tree and saw that more of the leaves had fallen, but many still were hanging on. I asked the Lord if He was going to send another earthquake to shake the rest of the leaves off the tree. He said, "No".

Symbolically, I believe this tree was a picture of us hanging on to old things or dead leaves of our own. He wants us to choose to let go of our dead leaves, to <u>exchange new for old and life for death</u>. He wants us to be a blank canvas on which He can paint His new life through us...His abundant re-creation.

He reminded me of:
Isa 61:3
To grant those who mourn in Zion, giving them a **garland** instead of ashes, the **oil of gladness** instead of mourning, the **mantle of praise** instead of a spirit of fainting. So they will be called **oaks of righteousness**, the planting of the LORD, **that He may be glorified.**

This verse speaks of exchanging good for bad and life for death...then being transformed into oaks (enduring and powerful trees) of righteousness.

Letting go of dead things in our lives is difficult because these things were once living; just as the leaves were once green and new. God ordained the existence of these things in our lives at one point. God gave them life, but now we may have to leave them behind in order to see new growth. We have to let go of the mindset that tells us to keep things going just because God gave birth to them once upon a time. What was once new, beautiful and healthy may be dying. The old, dead leaves must be gathered and thrown into the yard debris in favor of a new move of God in our lives. As fresh manna had to be gathered daily, so our intimacy with the Lord must be renewed each morning.

Our dead leaves could be old accomplishments and successes. We may need to let go of the roles that we have played in other's lives like moving from mentor to peer. The leaves could be long held attitudes that we have had that are now being challenged by the Holy Spirit Himself. He may be requiring us to yield to new revelation and understanding. How can we reach out to new revelation if we rigidly hang onto the past?

As a corporate body the leaves may be attitudes of faithlessness, pretenses or caring more about image than who the Lord is calling us to be; or possibly the dead acts of selfishness, laziness in prayer, unwillingness to serve or spiritual ambition. If our Lord is calling our body to a 'new thing', we will miss it if our eyes will not see His future because we would rather focus on the past.

<u>Now, Life:</u>

Then in the dream the Lord asked me, "Why does the oak tree still stand when the other trees have fallen?"

I looked and noticed that the uprooted trees had meager root balls compared to the height of the tree itself. And their small undeveloped root system could not support the height and weight of the tree when the earth shook.

The Lord then seemed to take me under the ground to observe the root system of the oak tree. It was vast. The roots were deep and wide. The oak tree's roots mimicked the branches in their scale and mass above the ground. As full, wide and high as the branches reached, so the roots stretched equally under ground.

Then the Lord said that He causes the growth to be accomplished first underground. In secret He builds the root system of our lives so that when the shaking comes, *and it will come*, we will remain standing. This is the process of building character, and it never ends. Though to others it may seem that we have little growth because the branches may be sparse and foliage even less developed, still He looks under the ground and proclaims our growth as good and steady.

I must confess I am often in a hurry for the things of God to come to pass in my family and my own life. When the Lord builds character, He is slow and methodical. He doesn't rush. Time is in His hands, and He is never anxious. Sometimes I wish I could move the hand of God, but then I remember the tall strong evergreen with the tiny root system and I remember that He knows what's best for me. He is taking His time to make you and me into the people that will remain standing even in the storms, floods and the earthquakes. God is kind and severe. But He is good!

## Gayle M. Nelson

If you have ever read 'The Chronicles of Narnia' by C.S. Lewis, you will remember when Mrs. Beaver explained to Lucy about the character of Aslan the Great Lion. This small child wondered if Aslan was safe. The answer was, "Aslan is not safe. He is not a tame lion. But He is good." Aslan represented Jesus in these stories. Jesus hates sin but loves us. He came as a lamb, but returns as a man of war with a sword coming out of His mouth and fire in His eyes. He's not a helpless little babe; He is the King of Kings. And He died to bring an end to the sting of death forever, so that we can truly live. Yes! He is good! But we can never accurately describe Him as safe!

Death is often such a frightening thing to us. We don't understand the mystery of it or comprehend the loss it brings. I don't want to minimize the pain of it, but we can trust Him. So the next time His severe mercy asks you to let something that you love die, try to remember His love truly is limitless and He will never leave us forsaken with grief.

Recently my husband and I experienced a type of death. The Lord led us to leave the only church we have known as Christians. We were members there for close to thirty years. We served in a leadership capacity for twenty of those years and grew to deeply love the people in that body. They were truly our family and we were happily knitted together with them.

For approximately five years, the Lord was speaking to us about leaving. We wrestled with that decision. It was not easy to leave. In fact we fought against it for most of that time. We didn't want to leave because we had invested our whole lives into that body. When He made it clear to us that it was time for us to leave, He gave me a vision as confirmation. I saw Wade and I standing in a field. We were holding a walking stick. The Lord said we needed to let go of what we had before He could give us something else. He was asking us to let go of our church family, our position, our comfort and our goals in that place. Not because those things were wrong. It was simply the season of Fall at that time in that place.

We needed to be stripped of everything that we knew and trust the Lord for new growth. It was hard and we didn't pass every test perfectly… and we are still learning. We mourn the loss of intimacy with the people there…because even if you try to maintain the relationships, people drift apart…often forgotten. We fought against that, but to no avail. However, God is patient and kind to continue guiding us.

Everything that can be shaken will be shaken…but God remains. His loving kindness is everlasting. And the <u>Prince of Peace is **faithful**</u>.

Isa 54:10
"For the mountains may be removed and <u>the hills may shake, but My lovingkindness will not be removed from you, and **My covenant of peace will not be shaken**</u>," says the LORD who has compassion on you

## THE KEY OF ASKING PERMISSION TO SPEAK

Since the Lord uses prophecy to speak to His body, then He should get to choose if, when and/or how we speak this cryptic, often mystical language.

2 Pet 1:20-21
20 But know this first of all, that no prophecy of Scripture is a matter of one's own interpretation,
21 for **no prophecy was ever made by an act of human will**, but men moved by the Holy Spirit spoke from God.

During the renewal in the mid 90's, my husband and I used to go to a lot of prayer meetings. It was a blast. God always was doing something exciting! One of those times, a few of us were praying for some folks. I was very new to functioning in the prophetic. And I made a lot of mistakes… this time I made a big mistake.

We were praying for a young man. Suddenly, I began crying. It started out small and I could control it. But pretty soon I was sobbing. I didn't know why I was so disturbed, so I asked the Lord to tell me. He did. He started telling me how desperately lonely and condemned this man felt. How he didn't know how much the Lord loved him. There was such heaviness. It was as though the Lord was grieving over him. It seemed to me that the Lord was eager to release him. So I said, "You have no idea how much the Lord loves you. He loves you more deeply than you could ever imagine". Then I couldn't talk any more because I was extremely overwhelmed.

Now, let me ask you something. Doesn't that message from God seem like a good message? I thought that it would be wonderful to know the riches of God's love. But that is not how it was received. Immediately this man looked at me and said, "Well, that's just great. Now I don't even know that God loves me? I can't do anything right. Now He's even telling me that I don't know how to be loved!"

The mood of the room drastically changed. My tears dried and I sat there dumbfounded. What had I done? I had chased the Holy Spirit away. I had quenched His movement in this poor man's life.

At this meeting there was another man who was like a mentor in the prophetic to some people at our church. I saw him at church the next day. Our eyes met as we made our way to the back of the church. I blurted out, "Who was I hearing if it wasn't the Lord? How could I have been so deceived that I didn't even know who was talking to me? What did I do wrong? Please help me."

He looked at me and said, "Gayle, it's not that you didn't hear the Lord. But, did you ask the Father if you could tell His child what He was telling you about him?". "No. I thought if God was saying something nice, it was OK to speak it out. I didn't know that even a sweet word could wound someone."

He then told me about the Lord's perfect timing for everything, and that not all 'words' are meant to be spoken. He is a great Dad and He knows what will help and what will hurt His own kids.

I learned an important lesson at the expense of somebody who was already wounded.

At times I have been so excited to "know" what God was saying that I have spoken too quickly. <u>Speaking before asking the Lord's permission is spiritual pride and it hurts people</u>. When I consider that fact, I wish that I could stop talking again. But I know He has called us to grow with Him and not hide from instruction. I just keep asking the Lord to help me to not hurt His kids. God's motivation is always love, restoration and freedom. My motivations must surrender to His, and then I hope I will learn and remember that each 'word' or whisper is His to do with what He wills for the good of His family. He gets to choose!

## **THE KEY OF THE WEIGHT OF SIN**

Isa. 53:4-6   The Message
But the fact is, it was *our* pains he carried— *our* disfigurements, all the things wrong with *us*. We thought he brought it on himself, that God was punishing him for his own failures. But it was our sins that did that to him, that ripped and tore and crushed him—*our sins*! He took the punishment, and that made us whole. Through his bruises we get healed. We're all like sheep who've wandered off and gotten lost. We've all done our own thing, gone our own way. And GOD has piled all our sins, everything we've done wrong, on him, on him.

I was fifteen years old when I received Jesus as my Lord and Savior. I wasn't ready to make that decision because I didn't understand what I was doing. But it was a happy day for my sister. She used to witness to me all of the time. And I was just awful to her. Part of me thought she was full of hot air. The other part hoped what she was saying was true, but I didn't really believe it.

So, in order to find out if this 'Jesus Stuff' was the real thing, I tested her. Secretly, I hoped that she would pass my tests. Regularly I pushed her to her limits. I tried to get her to lose her patience with me and yell or say a 'bad' word. I even tried to get her to fall in front of all her 'Jesus' friends. Yea, I was a real brat to her. Still, she continued to witness of God's love for me. Finally she wore me down. I promised to 'pray the prayer' if she would get off my back! She promised that she would. So, I repeated after her the sinner's prayer. At that time we slept in the same room and after we prayed she fell asleep. I, however, did not. That night was one of the worst nights of my life. I cried all night. I kept thinking when the sun came up, I would feel better. I cried more that night than I had in my whole life up to that point. Salt tracks ran down my face and I was dehydrated. Finally, I saw the sun start to rise and I realized that I didn't feel any better; in fact, I felt worse. From my bed, I whispered to God, 'If this is what it's like to give my life to You, forget it. I change my mind.' Then for the first time in my life, I was aware of Him speaking to me.

He said, "I let you feel a tiny bit of the weight of your sin for one night. Now do you know that you need Me?"

Stunned, I thought, "That was just a little bit of the weight of my own sin?" It was so overwhelming to me. I bore a tiny bit of that weight for just one night and I couldn't begin to endure it. I still haven't fully grasped what that all means and how massive my need for Him is, but I could finally pray and mean it. "Oh God, I'm such an idiot! Yes Lord, I do need You!"

Now when I see someone acting foolishly like I did, I can't help but wonder how the Lord will reveal their need to them. I pray they will hear Him calling them. But I know it's different for all of us. And I'm grateful that we all matter to Him so much. He tailors His approach to each of us. We are individual members of His body and each of us is valuable enough to touch one by one. What's so remarkable that He is interested in each heart. His grace truly is amazing!

## THE KEY OF PLAYING WITH THE FATHER

Zeph 3:17
"The LORD your God is in your midst, a victorious warrior. **He will exult over you with joy,** He will be quiet in His love, **He will <u>rejoice over you</u> with shouts of joy**.

Did you know that in the Strongs Concordance the word (rejoice) means to **spin around**. It also means to be under the influence of violent or explosive emotions. The Lord wants to dance, spin around and PLAY with us! He's a fun Dad!!!

My earthly dad wasn't a strong believer when I was growing up. He was a devout Catholic and a very moral man, but he didn't have an intimacy with the Lord. If I was to examine every thing he did, he might not be judged the best dad in the world. However, there was one thing that I just love to remember about my dad. He was such a kid at heart. He loved presents. It could be anything. You could wrap up a box of dirt and he would still be thrilled that you thought enough about him to tease him.

If he liked you, he would give you a nick-name. My nick-name was (I can't believe I'm going to tell you...) Baby Guitz! My siblings were nick-named: Strick-Nine Annie, Big Shot, Grantsis has ants in his pantsis, Leany Eyes or Laughing Eyes and Briny Googal Dandy wants some peas and candy. There's a little window into my childhood.

Taking us swimming or to the park to play softball; or to swing on the swings was the kind of thing my dad liked to do sometimes. And when he wanted to go, he would sneak up behind us and whisper, 'Hey, lets go have some fun!' Or he might come and surprise us saying, 'I'm gonna go to the park. Ya wanna come?' Or maybe after swimming, he'd say, 'Let's get some ice cream! Who wants ice cream?'

In the morning when he shaved he would have a lot of lather on his face and chase us around the living room saying that he wanted a kiss. We would all run away squealing.

Much later, after I was married and had two kids, my dad used to come and visit. I would open the door to find him standing there saying gruffly, "Hey, ya got any coffee?" I would invite him in for coffee and he would tell me about his day. Then often he would take Jered with him on errands. My dad and my son were very close. In fact, I think that my dad was closer to Jered than he was with any of his own children, including me. It made me feel closer to him knowing how much he loved to spend time with Jered. Jered called him, 'Bompa' and my dad called him 'little guy'. They were the best of friends.

During the renewal, I experienced the love of the father more than I ever had in my whole Christian life up to that point. It seemed that He poured out buckets of love on His kids. We got to play with our Dad. It was so sweet. And many times during that particular time frame, I could hear Him in my spirit say, "Hey I'm gonna have some fun. You wanna come?" People were laughing, falling down, crying and dancing with great joy. He was having fun! He was having all that fun with us, His kids.

To me that's what the renewal was all about. A lot of people got hung up with the controversies, arguing about the manifestations, complaining about how people were faking some of it or all of it. It really wasn't that deep! It wasn't about theology or deeper wisdom. Dad was asking us to play and some of us said, "YES"! We got to experience our heavenly Father lavishing His great love on His kids. Now when He asks me join Him in whatever He is up to, I can't wait. Because hanging out with Dad is great! He always has something exciting or challenging happening. Our Dad is full of adventure…and I think that He loves it when we want to go with Him.

## THE KEY OF FAITH vs. HIS SOVEREIGNTY

I have been struggling with a sickness called Lupus (sorry to bring it up so much but these trials helped in my instruction) for most of my life. But more than a personal health problem, the wrestling match I was engaged in centered on God's ability vs. His willingness.

The 'faith' books encourage us to believe that God does and will heal people. The writers often tell us that if we aren't experiencing healing, our faith is deficient in some way. They say, 'Just claim it and it will be done'. The Lord is our healer, He is faithful and He will bring it to pass.

Exod 15:26
And He said, "If you will give earnest heed to the voice of the LORD your God, and do what is right in His sight, and give ear to His commandments, and keep all His statutes, I will put none of the diseases on you which I have put on the Egyptians; for **I, the LORD, am your healer**."

Ps 103:3
Who pardons all your iniquities; **who heals all your diseases**;

Isa 53:4
Surely our **griefs He himself bore**, and our **sorrows He carried**; yet we ourselves esteemed Him stricken, smitten of God, and afflicted.

I must confess for most of my Christian life, this key of faith/sovereignty has eluded me. I've been prayed for and anointed for the purpose of healing more times than I can count by more people than I could ever list. I said I believed but I almost always doubted. I thought since God could turn something meant for bad to the good, that sickness could be a good thing.

But Jesus suffered and died so that I could be free if I would only believe. He didn't suffer for Himself! He had no sin. He had no sickness. He did it for me and for you because He loves us. But I did not fully embrace His word until recently.

1 Pet 2:24

and He Himself bore our sins in His body on the cross, that we might die to sin and live to righteousness; for **by His wounds you <u>WERE</u> healed**.

Isa 53:5
But He was pierced through for our transgressions, He was crushed for our iniquities; the chastening for our well-being fell upon Him, and **by His scourging we <u>ARE</u> healed**.

For over thirty years, I had Lupus, or more accurately – Lupus had me. There is no cure. It was time to take a RISK. The only thing I had that was big enough to prove the reality of my faith was my life.

<u>**C. S. Lewis, "Only real risk tests the reality of a belief."**</u>

So I put all of my eggs in the 'faith' basket. I prayed and confessed my healing in the same manner that I prayed and confessed my salvation.

Rom 10:8-11
8  But what does it say? "The word is near you, in your mouth and in your heart"-- that is, the word of faith which we are preaching,
9  that if you **confess with your mouth** Jesus as Lord, and believe in your heart that God raised Him from the dead, you shall be <u>**saved**</u>;
10  for with the heart man believes, resulting in righteousness, **and with the mouth he <u>confesses</u>, resulting in salvation.**
11  For the Scripture says, "Whoever believes in Him will not be disappointed."

**At the cross, He saved me wholly. Not just salvation from sin, but disease and sickness too**. It's as simple as that. Maybe I was simply making this whole healing thing too hard.

In the past, I had some questions that kept me from believing that God would heal me. People who prayed for me often told me to thank God for my healing and 'confess' that I was healed. I routinely refused because that seemed like lying to me. After all, I didn't 'feel' any different and I had no scientific proof of my healing. But they would always tell me that I should do it anyway. I of course asked, 'WHY?' They said it was in the Bible. 'Where', I queried. No real answer was ever given, at least any that I could understand. I wanted to be TRUE. To speak, live and do the truth.

One day during this time of deliverance and instruction (which continues even now) the Lord spoke to my heart. "You are so concerned with the truth. What is truer than My Word?" I realized then there was <u>nothing</u> more true than His Word. How I felt, what I thought was true or even what the test results stated didn't even come close to the TRUTH of His Word.

Romans 10:8-11 promises <u>that if we believe and CONFESS we will be saved! We must always believe before the promise comes to pass.</u> Abraham believed and obeyed first, then, when human provision was impossible, God accomplished His promise. Noah believed and obeyed and eventually saw the provision and progression of the word of the Lord. Daniel believed a word of promise from seventy years prior and labored in prayer under great opposition to see the hand of God move. Joseph believed and obeyed faithfully until the promise of the Lord was accomplished in his life that affected the whole nation. These men of old confessed their belief with their actions. Their very lives CONFESSED the truth of God. In this scripture, the confession of faith led to salvation. The word 'saved' is the same word that Jesus used when He healed people in their bodies and saved their souls.

4982  sozo (sode'-zo);
from a primary sos (contraction for obsolete saoz, "safe"); to save, i.e. deliver or protect (literally or figuratively):
KJV-- **heal**, preserve, **save** (self), do well, be (make) whole.

Many places in the Bible use sozo (saved and healed). That word is used to show when Jesus healed from sickness and when He saved from sin. That's why, when the paralyzed man was brought to Jesus, He initially said that his sins were forgiven. Forgiveness from sin or freedom from sin is the same thing as being free from sickness. Both were accomplished on the cross.

<u>RISK</u>: On the basis of the scriptures before, I confessed my healing. I gradually stopped taking my medications (there were many). I began to share my testimony of healing. Wade and I WHOLLY embraced this healing and we left NO room for anything else. I was convinced that unless I

was 'sold out' to this position of faith, my healing would not be realized.

I was met with skepticism, ridicule and questions from family, some friends and medical professionals. You wouldn't think that faith would be seen as controversial, but it was. I suppose people were just concerned for me.

Finally I was off all of the medications. I had been tethered to those drugs for over twenty years. It felt great to be free. I was happy and excited to live a new life. I don't think that I can adequately convey how truly wonderful it felt to be completely off those drugs for the first time in a very long time.

Then gradually, my health began to slide downward. I tried to pretend that it wasn't happening. I began to challenge my body more and more to somehow prove my faith. My faith was not met with victory. The constant pain and fatigue soon overwhelmed me. In a matter of a couple of weeks, I was suffering a severe lupus flare-up. After so many years being tied to that medication 'leash', I thought that I might finally get to run free without the leash like a dog rambunctiously running in an open field. I was wrong. When I got to the point of being nearly incapacitated, I was forced to go back on the medications. I pinned my hope on God's ability with little if any thought to His perfect will and timing.

## I TRIED TO FORCE GOD INTO A BOX THAT LEFT NO ROOM FOR HIS SOVEREIGNTY!

But there is a huge problem with this approach. GOD IS SOVEREIGN! He is my master. And I am not simply His slave, I am His bond slave. (Bond slave defined in the introduction)

Can God heal? Absolutely! Will God always heal? Positionally, YES. By His stripes we WERE healed.

This is the point at which my personal wrestling match begins and ends. Maybe healing is like sanctification. We know we are justified by faith… yet we work out our salvation with fear and trembling. As we yield daily to the Lord, we are transformed more and more into His image. Sanctification is a miracle that doesn't happen in a moment; it is a life-long process.

I still believe God can and does heal. I also still believe that He will heal me. But ultimately, whether He does or does not, I am His. I choose to live according to His supremacy with gratitude because no matter what my circumstances, He is good! I need only look at the cross to understand that fact. But at the same time, this trial feels like a weight from which I will never be free. Writing about it makes me feel exposed…filleted. We can live in obedience and still be wounded in spirit. So, while I choose to serve the Lord no matter what…I'm hopeful He will rescue me from this weight.

On another front regarding the Lord's sovereignty, Wade and I are in yet another wrestling match. As I mentioned before, we were members of our previous church for almost thirty years and were in leadership for twenty of those years. The Lord asked us to leave. So we did. Now we feel at loose ends. We struggle in the in-between. The jail cell waiting for release…the back side of the desert…we wait…wondering if we wasted our time for thirty years. My heart tells me that we didn't…but my head isn't always so sure about that.

Again we are confronted with the answer that God is in charge of our lives. And for His sake, we live and move and have our being.

How do I live this faith He has given me? How do I balance His ability with my lack? How do I live a life of freedom tethered to my sick bed? How do we embrace the future while waiting in jail?

These are the mysteries that I can't seem to comprehend. I am left to conclude that without the Lord's provision, my biggest hopes are simply wishful thoughts. He is the only one that can bring healing. I can't make it happen independent of God. I guess I'm just trying to be real with this 'key'. It's the hardest one to write about because it feels like I have no place to hide and I can't find the lock to insert this key.

Ps 127:1
**Unless the LORD builds the house, they labor in vain who build it**; unless the LORD guards the city, the watchman keeps awake in vain.

Clearly, I don't fully understand the issue of faith vs. the sovereignty of God. I may never grasp it. But I do know that we can know <u>Him</u> better.

We can allow Him to transform us day by day into His image.

2 Cor 3:16-18
16 but whenever a man turns to the Lord, the veil is taken away.
17 Now the Lord is the Spirit; and where the Spirit of the Lord is, there is liberty.
18 But we all, with unveiled face beholding as in a mirror the glory of the Lord, are being <u>transformed into the same image from glory to glory</u>, just as from the Lord, the Spirit.

Before I began again to take the medications, I was asked many times by various medical professionals why I stopped taking the medications. With tears I asked them if they had ever been forced to take drugs. Most said, 'No'. My answer was that they could never really know the discouragement of it. If I had no faith or great hope, it probably wouldn't be so hard. I would reconcile myself to this life with no hopes being continuously dashed. But, being so completely invested in believing God enough to risk your very life can't really be explained adequately to someone who does not possess the same hope. As you read this, if you don't understand my struggle…My hope is that experientially at least, you never will.

## **THE KEY OF A NAME CHANGE LEADING TO A CHARACTER CHANGE**

Gen 32:28
And he said, "Your name shall no longer be Jacob, but Israel; for you have striven with God and with men and have prevailed."

Shortly after the renewal started, in about the mid 90s, the Lord started engaging me in a conversation about who I was and who I was meant to be. My name, Gayle, means happy. The Lord impressed on me that I could be more than just happy. <u>I could be Joy</u>. My nature could be changed into someone who exudes joy instead of skepticism and cynicism; someone who didn't rely on happenings to be happy. This was very intriguing to me. Imagine with me how extraordinary it would be to have GOD'S JOY that knows no bounds in all situations. No matter if things were going well or badly, I could live His joy. A joy that came directly from His heart and was delivered to mine, that wasn't some false feeling I conjured up to make me appear happy. I know you know this but let me make sure we are on the same page.

Being joy-full doesn't mean being happy all of the time. Strong's Concordance describes 'joy' as being calmly delighted. And not delighted in a goofy way, but a joyful satisfaction in God's provision and will in all circumstances. It is something that we can actually possess whether circumstances make us 'feel' happy or sad. What a gold mine!

I realize this is something God offers every believer, but I had never seriously taken Him up on His offer. In order to receive this 'gold mine', I needed to change my mind about how I looked at things. And I guess I wasn't ready to do that until I reached the point; the point in my Christian life that I was ready to admit that I had been wrong about life, God, and how He wants me to live the life He gave me. I had to change before I could receive Him in this way.

So I asked the Lord to help me. I suppose that was an obvious first step... since I hadn't been able to do it on my own.

Isa 55:8-9
8 "For My thoughts are not your thoughts, neither are your ways My ways," declares the LORD.
9 "For as the heavens are higher than the earth, so are **My ways higher than your ways, and My thoughts than your thoughts.**

The Lord and I spent months on this issue. And to be honest with you, I'm a bit slow because I still don't have this down. On my own I tend to be fatalistic and kind of negative. Thank the Lord He is patient. We used to sing a song in the choir (a million years ago). I think it was called, 'Please be patient with me...God is not through with me yet'.

Anyway, after several months, the women in charge of 'women's ministry' were planning an intercession /prophetic training retreat. I was asked to come and help out.

The night before the retreat I had a dream. In the dream, I had just arrived at the retreat. As I walked into the main room, a bunch of women called to me. But they didn't call me by my name. They all called me Joy. In the dream, the fact that they were calling me 'Joy' didn't seem odd because it really was my name.

I woke up and got ready to go to the retreat. I didn't really think about the dream. It seemed insignificant to me.

The first night we worshipped and prayed and had some instruction regarding intercession, and then we prayed some more. Most of us stayed up and talked for a while and then went to bed...or should I say 'went to sleeping bags'. The next day we did retreat stuff until the evening session. Then we broke into small groups. The purpose of the groups was to give women an opportunity to practice their prophetic gifts. I was helping out a leader of one of these groups. So, most of the time I was looking for openings to encourage these women so that they could move from immature prophetic giftings to more mature. And I was there just in case things got out of order...you know, like being a cop in charge of crowd control!

About a half-hour into it, a woman looked up at me. She had a very confused look on her face. 'Are you OK?' I asked. She said that she had heard something in her spirit but that it couldn't be right...she must be crazy or something. I told her that it often feels like that in the beginning and asked her to tell us what she had heard.

She said she thought that God was telling her my name was Joy. But she was sure she must have heard wrong because she had asked the leader what my name was and it was Gayle.

**<u>"Have I got a story for you!"</u>** And I began to tell all of them what the Lord and I had been talking about. So, we both got to be encouraged by the Lord. God's so funny sometimes. **<u>He was showing me that He had changed my identity to JOY!</u>**

Around the same time, I saw a great change in a friend of mine. He has been a close friend for at least twenty years now and was also my boss for part of that time.

I have almost always viewed him as a pastor/shepherd. During a trip to Toronto with a few people from his church, he had an amazing experience that changed him dramatically. I'm not sure of all the details but the Lord revealed to him that he was chosen by God to 'shepherd' His sheep. My friend had apparently never seen himself the way that many people saw him. I've always trusted his leading and willingly followed his advice, but for some reason he hadn't considered that as a true pastoring gift. But ever since that trip, he has taken the gifts that God has given him for His body seriously and faithfully shepherded all those that the Lord has given him.

I always thought he was a great guy. But now, he's even more amazing. He sees who the Lord has made him and he fully functions that way. He blesses all of us who benefit from the gift of God given freely through him.

God changed his image of himself into the image that God had created for him. He is a very honorable man…but now his heart is even more tender toward the Lord and His sheep.

## **THE KEY OF MIRACLES**

Mark 10:27
Looking upon them, Jesus said, **"With men it is impossible,** but not with God; **for all things are possible with God."**

I have seen people healed of cancer. I have witnessed marriages seemingly broken beyond repair restored. And I have personally received a measure of healing. But an even more amazing miracle happened to me.

It was about 1981. We were at church and the associate pastor was speaking. He was talking about forgiveness. He said that if we didn't forgive others then we would not be forgiven.

Matt 6:14-15
14 "For if you forgive men for their transgressions, your heavenly Father will also forgive you.
15 "But **if you do not forgive men, then your Father will not forgive your transgressions**.

Immediately the Holy Spirit convicted me. The Lord put His finger on an attitude of unforgiveness and possibly even hatred toward someone in my family.

Realizing that I needed to forgive and love him, I couldn't help but wonder how that was possible.  How could I remember without the 'sting' of pain that always came with the memory?  And how could I truly love someone while feeling that sting?  Was it possible to have my memory erased?  And if the memory was retained, could I still fully forgive him?

I was in the car with my husband on the way home.  Silently, I debated the issue with God.  "Lord, I know nothing is impossible for you.  But I don't think that I possess the faith required to fully forgive him.  **Can You change my mind?  Can you erase the pain?**"  I felt that the Lord said to my spirit, "Ask me for a miracle."

In my mind at the time, I thought cynically that it would take a miracle for me to obey Him in this.  But I decided the Lord would help me in any case, so I asked Him for the ability to obey Him and forgive from my heart without reservation.

A couple days later, my mom called me to ask for a favor.  This family member had been kicked out of his house, his wife wanted a divorce and he wanted a Bible.  My mom couldn't get away and she wanted me to take one to him.

Now let me give you a little background.  My memories begin at about six years of age.  I remember him being very cruel and abusive at times, especially when our parents would leave the house.  One time before my parents left for an evening out, I ran to my mom and I told her about all of the bad things that happened when they would leave.  I pleaded with her to stay and protect us or at least find someone else to watch over us.  She just laughed and said that I had an overactive imagination.

Before I write anything else you should know that none of us were believers at that time.  And it was a long time ago so this type of thing was not dealt with very well back then.

So the pattern that developed was as follows.  My parents would leave out the back door to get into the car.  As soon as they were gone, I made a mad dash to the front door.  If I got there first, I would run outside and hide in the neighborhood until they returned.  If I didn't make it to the door first, then 'he' would sometimes put me in the closet until our parents came home.  He didn't torture me or anything too dramatic, but it was scary to me.  And from inside the closet I could hear other things that were happening…things that were disturbing to me.

Growing up, I made it my goal to never be in the same room with that person. At a family function, if he went into the kitchen, I went to the living room…and on and on, room by room. I didn't believe he would hurt me…I just didn't trust him and that emotion made me feel afraid and out of control; just like when I was a child.

Back to the story…Here I was an adult being asked by my mom to not only go to his apartment but to go alone. I thought of every excuse I could, no matter how lame it sounded. "Oh, I wish I could mom, but I'm in the middle of something." "I don't have very much gas in the car." "I can't find an extra Bible and I don't have any cash." "There's no way that he's going to read the Bible! Give me a break!"

I finally realized I was not going to get out of this, so I put on my shoes and headed for his apartment, Bible in hand. When I got there I knocked but nobody came to the door. I thought, 'Oh God, you just wanted me to be willing. So now I can just leave the Bible here and go! Thank God!' But when I opened the screen door to put the Bible inside, he opened the front door.

He seemed really surprised to see me, but asked me to come in. "Oh, well, I can't. I was in the middle of something and I have to get back to it. You know how it is. Mom just wanted me to drop this off for you anyway. So, here's the Bible, you can keep it." He looked at me with the saddest face. He seemed to know that I didn't want anything to do with him. Then he said, "Couldn't you come in for just a minute? Please?" Before I knew it I was inside his apartment. The curtains were shut so it was really dark. The ashtrays were full and the smell of smoke was thick and made it hard to breathe. Empty beer bottles were all around and there were more than I could count with a glance. I sat down on the couch. The silence was deafening. I awkwardly tried to make some conversation. "I'm really sorry to hear that your marriage is in trouble. Hopefully you can work it out." "No. She's filing for divorce tomorrow," was his reply. "Gosh, that's too bad."

I couldn't stand it…I had to get out of there. So I stood up and said, "Well, if you need anything else just let me know. I guess I'll see you later." He stood up too and said in a really quiet voice, "I can't believe that you came. I thought you hated me. I was such an *** when we were growing up." I was on my way to the door when he said that, so I turned around and looked at him. His eyes were full of tears. I felt so bad for him…was that compassion? Did I actually feel compassion for 'him'? I just stood there and said, "Yea, things were pretty strange back then." Then he said it. The words I never expected to hear. "I'm so sorry. Can you forgive me?" Then my eyes filled with tears. Could I?

Even as I write this, I am overwhelmed. A little war was going on in my head that day. Its not that I didn't want to forgive him…it was just that I didn't believe it was possible. And I didn't want to say it if it wasn't true. I felt I owed him the truth at very least.

But then the miracle happened! It felt like a million little holes were poked into my heart and that all of the hatred and pain just leaked out of me. And then the love that I had reserved for 'more deserving' people leaked out too. I really cared about him. I wanted him to be free. I wanted him to know the Lord and have intimacy with Him forever. I couldn't believe it. I smiled at him and said, "Yes, I can forgive you because I know that the Lord has forgiven me. I'm the same as you. I need forgiveness too." He walked up to me and hugged me and miraculously, I hugged him back and told him that I loved him…and I really did and do.

I still remember all the things that happened to all of us growing up. But there is no pain. No hatred, bitterness or unforgiveness remain. It was impossible for me, but with God all things are possible. All I had to do was ask and be willing to let go.

Now we talk on the phone and he comes by and we hang out. We are actually friends. And I don't just love him, I like him too. God is so good! He performed a miracle for us and in us.

KEY summarization: all of the prior attitude adjustments that the Lord needed to make in me were for my good. I was stubborn and convinced that my way was the right way. The Lord was helping me to jump over a huge chasm between where my character was and where He had designed me to be. I needed His help to be more like Him. His ways are higher, better and worth learning and adopting. I am grateful for the mirror of Truth in His Word. He helped me to see myself…and see Him so that I could trust Him to change me from the inside out. His loving kindness <u>is</u> everlasting!

## Section II

## **FIGHTING THE GOOD FIGHT**

As we enter into battle with the Lord in intercession, we knit our hearts together with His. We connect with Him for His purposes; joining as one for the things that He is passionate about.

1 Tim 1:18-19
18 This command I entrust to you, Timothy, my son, **in accordance with the prophecies previously made concerning you, that by them you may fight the good fight,**
19 keeping faith and a good conscience, which some have rejected and suffered shipwreck in regard to their faith.

The following keys are about fighting against the strongholds that can keep us from realizing God's purposes for our lives. These strongholds are simply wrong or faithless ways of thinking that trap us in lives that are less than what we could be living.

A 'good conscience', as mentioned in 1Tim.1:18, 19, is important when fighting the 'good fight'. A heart free of bitterness, fear and faithlessness is critical to seeing the future hope realized. It's hard to see God's vision when the eyes of our heart are clouded with sin.

My husband and I have received many more words for our son than we have for our daughter. Friends, preachers, prophetic leaders and even strangers have given us 'words' regarding Jered's future. Many of them came when he was a child. We didn't understand it then, but now we do. These words are our weapons to fight for his future. We have not realized the promises of God regarding our son YET, but in the fullness of time (due time) we are confident that we will!

Gal 6:9
And let us not lose heart in doing good, for **in due time we shall reap** if we do not grow weary.

These are keys to help us hold onto the promises of God. If we can learn to implement them, we will be fit for battle and possess a pure heart toward the Lord.

## **THE KEY OF FIGHTING THE SPIRIT OF SUICIDE**

I heard Jack Deere recently say that Christians don't like to admit extreme emotions. For instance, they may not want to admit that they once hated someone. We're told that we should say we were bitter or unforgiving or something else that sounds more acceptable. He said you should just admit hate or whatever the sin is so that you could be completely free with repentance. After all, if you repent of hatred, chances are it will be easier to repent of 'lesser' sins and obtain forgiveness for all the other stuff as well. So in that vein of truth, I openly confess to being seduced by a spirit of suicide.

Jonah 4:8-9
8  And it came about when the sun came up that God appointed a scorching east wind, and the sun beat down on Jonah's head so **that he became faint and begged with all his soul to die, saying, "Death is better to me than life."**
9  Then God said to Jonah, "Do you have good reason to be angry about the plant?" And he said, "I have good reason to be angry, even to death."

Jonah was being pretty melodramatic, huh? This might seem like an odd scripture to put here. I think the reason I was led to it is because suicide is such a selfish desire. It is the ultimate escape, the ultimate self-indulgence. Self-pity and weakness seduces those who consider it. I know this because I was so seduced.

This seduction happened most dramatically twice. The first time I was in the hospital because I had overdosed. It was before I was prescribed painkillers. Wade was out of town and during those times I was particularly vulnerable to demonic attack.

The first night Wade was gone the enemy blasted me. The physical pain was so extreme I drank a whole bottle of wine (gasp!) and took a bunch of Tylenol. I was up all night because of the pain, so when morning came I fed the kids, took them to school and called my best friend and told her what I had done. I further told her that I was finally going to bed and asked if she would pick up the kids and not let them come home, just in case I didn't wake up. I was very calm and matter of fact about it. She of course was not! Her husband came and banged on my bedroom window until I woke up; he then took me to the hospital. I was told that it was almost too late to save my liver and kidneys.

During that hospital stay, I was continually asked by a variety of doctors if I was trying to kill myself. I scoffed at the question. "Of course I wasn't trying to kill myself. Don't be ridiculous!" Then a friend I hadn't seen in years visited me. She said that the Lord had sent her to talk to me. She brought her Bible and opened it up.

Rom 8:35-39
35 Who shall separate us from the love of Christ? Shall tribulation, or distress, or persecution, or famine, or nakedness, or peril, or sword?
36 Just as it is written, "For Thy sake we are being put to death all day long; we were considered as sheep to be slaughtered."
37 But in all these things <u>we overwhelmingly conquer through Him</u> who loved us.
38 **For I am convinced that neither death, <u>NOR LIFE</u>**, nor angels, nor principalities, nor things present, nor things to come, nor powers,
39 nor height, nor depth, nor any other created thing, shall be able to separate us from the love of God, which is in Christ Jesus our Lord.

After she read the above scripture, she looked at me with surprise and said, "You aren't afraid of death, but 'life' separating you from the Lord!" In that instant, I felt like a load of bricks had been dropped on me. It was true. I didn't fear death, I feared living and falling away. I was afraid that I might fall away from the Lord because in the midst of suffering, I had begun to question His love and care for me. I was beginning to resent Him for 'allowing' the enemy to get me with the physical pain. I had more faith in the Devil's ability to deceive me than God's ability to keep me in Him. I of course needed to repent of that glaring lack of faith…but I must admit that it was hard to go to the place of repentance.

After I returned home, I asked a counselor friend to come over. I explained what had happened. I was still a little confused…was I really suicidal? She walked me through some healing but it wasn't complete. I considered suicide as weakness and couldn't see myself that way because of my prideful hard heart.

I was on guard against that weakness for a long time, and then I fell again. It was years later. The Lupus was much worse, and I was prescribed three painkillers. One night I lay in bed with tears running down the sides of my face. The pain was extreme. Shaking uncontrollably, I had taken all the medication that I dare take. Still the pain was far beyond me. 'Momentary light affliction' seemed like anything but momentary! I prayed for relief but none came. The enemy began the seduction. "God's not going to rescue you. And you aren't strong enough to handle it this time. Why should you suffer? He obviously doesn't care about you. You can be free of this…you know how…go ahead. If He won't rescue you, rescue yourself!" his forked tongue hissed.

I can not adequately describe how I longed to rescue myself. Not ten feet from my bedroom door sat the *answer to my problem*. The *'key'* to my freedom and relief was within reach. I had more than enough drugs to be free. It would have been so easy…and this pain was so hard to endure… why should I? WHY SHOULD I WAIT FOR RELIEF THAT NEVER COMES?

Then I heard it. He called out my name. It wasn't audible, but to me it sounded like He was SCREAMING it in me head.
  "GAYLE……………….GAYLE! Return….Repent…extract the precious from the worthless."

Jer 15:19
Therefore, thus says the LORD, "**If you return, then I will restore you**-- Before Me you will stand; and if you **extract the precious from the worthless**, you will become My spokesman. They for their part may turn to you, but as for you, you must not turn to them.

 As is so often the case, I had to choose. Will I seek relief for myself and ignore the Lord and His call to me? Will I look to others for sympathy and support to the exclusion of God? Or will I repent and choose to see the precious? Is THIS the day that the Lord has made? To myself I asked, "Doesn't He deserve worship and praise whether I'm having a good day OR NOT?" YES He does! But how do I rise above 'pain'?

I'm not going to lie. That night continued to be just horrible. But I'm still here weeding through the worthless looking for the precious. My testimony is that God is good…All the time…God is good! But I also must admit that I am frail of heart and mind and am, at times, easily beguiled.

1 Pet 5:8-9
8 Be of sober spirit, be on the alert. Your adversary, the devil, prowls about like a roaring lion, seeking someone to devour.
9 But resist him, firm in your faith, knowing that the same experiences of suffering are being accomplished by your brethren who are in the world.

Since those days, I have experienced a measure of freedom from the physical pain (mostly through medication). But I am aware that if the enemy could cause me to believe a lie about God and His goodness once, he could tempt me to believe it again. His tactics don't really change. I think the Devil always wants us to question God's love and care for us.

2 Cor 2:11
in order that no advantage be taken of us by Satan; for <u>we are not ignorant of his schemes</u>.

The enemy is always scheming to isolate us, convincing us our struggles are unique. Wade and I have made some changes to safe guard my body and soul when he is away. Wade will tell those we trust that he will be traveling and prepares prayer cover for me in his absence. This wisdom has been a great protection for me. I know that I am not alone in this and if you have ever struggled in this way, you aren't alone either.

We all have trials and challenges in this life. But even in the 'dark' days we can find our treasures in the Lord.

Isa 45:3
"And **I will give you the <u>treasures of darkness</u>, and hidden wealth of secret places, in order that you may know that <u>it is I, the LORD</u>, the God of Israel, <u>who calls you by your name.</u>**

He called me by my name. He called me out of the darkness of fear and pain into the secret place of hidden wealth, the place where faith isn't a theory or a discussion topic. He is calling all of us to a place in our own hearts where we can actually plumb the depths of God.

1 Cor 2:7-10
7 but **we speak God's wisdom in a mystery, the <u>hidden wisdom</u>**, which

God predestined before the ages to our glory;
8 the wisdom which none of the rulers of this age has understood; for if they had understood it, they would not have crucified the Lord of glory;
9 but just as it is written, "<u>Things which eye has not seen and ear has not heard, and which have not entered the heart of man, all that God has prepared for those who love Him.</u>"
10 For to us God revealed them through the Spirit; for **the Spirit searches all things, even the depths of God.**

To know Him more fully is worth a great price. That's why He is referred to as a pearl of great price. But knowing Him will cost us. A valuable treasure is not easily found or stumbled upon. We must honestly confront ourselves with the question, "<u>Do I really want to sacrifice to fully KNOW Him?</u>" Make an honest evaluation of yourself. Be brutally frank, because it is very expensive to truly KNOW His heart…and it may cost you your very life!

Matt. 10:38, 39
38 And he who does not take his cross and follow after Me is not worthy of Me,
39 He who has found his life will lose it, and he who has lost his life for My sake will find it.

In my weakest moments, I have envied the lives around me that seem somehow easier. Maybe these other Christians have their health, faithful and healthy children, financial and ministry success. When I let myself sink into the mire of self pity, I've wished that I had the 'easy' life. It is so subjective. I am sure some people view my marriage and wish they had that kind of 'oneness' with their spouse. So before He requires me to repent of my envious attitude, He whispers the question, "Do you trust Me?" And I, like Peter, have to answer honestly, "To whom else shall I go…only You have the keys to eternal life."

## THE KEY OF THE VALUE OF INTERCESSION

Heb 7:25
Therefore he is able to save completely those who come to God through him, because **he always lives to <u>intercede</u> for them**. (NIV)

I was coming back home after having spent the day at the capital doing some political work. I decided to go to a Bible study about intercession. I knew very little experientially about it back then. A friend of mine was hosting the meeting at her house so I figured that it was time I learned. Having come from work, I arrived late, so I sat in the back with my friend. All the people were from the same church except for me. As I sat and listened to the teacher, I was stunned when she stopped and pointed at me. She said the Lord had told her that He was 'positioning' me for something new. Later she came up to me and asked if that meant anything to me. I said I thought it was interesting that she would use the word 'positioning' because that's a political term we use regularly. She said that she had never had the Lord use that word prophetically through her before.

I wasn't able to attend all of the meetings, but began a relationship with the teacher of the class. After a while she organized an intercessory team to pray for a legislator (who attended her church) and me. This is how the Lord chose to teach me about intercession. I learned what it was like to be carried in prayer and conversely, I learned what it felt like to be dropped. I could actually sense when they were or weren't praying for me.

I will never minimize the power of true intercessors again. It isn't just praying for someone, it is laying down your life for them. It is standing between where they are and where they will be and calling that change into being. It requires great faith and faithfulness. Intercession requires maturity beyond self-interest. <u>I aspire to the level of grace that sees prophetically what an individual will be in the kingdom of God</u>. The reason that I want to see prophetically what the Lord is calling them to is because I hope to be part of their freedom. He has given us a hope and a future, and hearing the Lord's plans for someone's future is the objective of desiring the prophetic gift and calling into being the plans of God.

1 Cor 14:1
Pursue love, yet **desire earnestly** spiritual gifts, but especially **that you may prophesy**.

Having committed intercession on my behalf changed me. Now I can value something I had not understood because those people gave so unselfishly to me. The Lord continued to teach me about intercession through other opportunities.

## Gayle M. Nelson

One night I was being tormented through physical pain. The pain had become a common experience, but rarely had a tormenting spirit accompanied it. I lay awake unable to sleep and I began to see a vision. It was beautiful at first. Lovely ribbons of metallic colors swirling around like waves of color flowing in the breeze. Then they began to take shape; frightening shapes of warring demons. It was graphic in its violence and gore. I tried to close my eyes, but even then I could see that terrible scene. There seemed to be no escape. So, I cried out to the Lord. But still I saw it with my eyes open and closed. I didn't know what to do and suddenly I had the thought to ask for the intercessors to pray. It was the middle of the night so I didn't think that I should call someone, so I cried out loud, 'Wake up the intercessors, Lord! Wake them to pray!!!' This was at about 4:00am. About ten minutes after I prayed that prayer I was at peace. The attack ended and I fell asleep.

The next day a friend of mine called and asked what had happened to me in the middle of the night. I asked her what she meant. She said that at about 4:00am she woke up to seeing two hands around a mouth forming a kind of a megaphone yelling, 'WAKE UP!' She sat up and started to pray for me. She said she just somehow knew that she was supposed to pray for me. In about ten minutes it was over and she went back to sleep.

When I remember that night, I am incredibly humbled that the Lord would do that for me. I am also amazed at the willingness of my friend. She didn't ask God to explain, she simply obeyed. She is an intercessor that knows without question the power of God in prayer.

The next instance began at church. We were sitting in the back, as we often did, and I saw a man. His name, and the fact that our daughter had baby-sat for his children, was all that I knew about him. When I looked at him, I thought I heard the Lord say He was going to 'free' him that night. That seemed nice to know, but I didn't give it much thought until the end of the service. Our pastor gave an alter call for freedom! I sat there thanking the Lord for freeing this man and I peeked at him to see if he was raising his hand. He didn't. Our pastor asked for the prayer ministry to go down to the altar to pray for people, so we went. After praying for a few people, I noticed he was still sitting in his seat. I figured that I had not heard the Lord correctly. But then the Lord said it again. He wanted to free this man. So, I had a little wrestling match with the Lord. What was I supposed to do? I didn't even know him. Have you ever felt like the Lord had his foot against the small of your back? It's as though with one quick thrust He could hurl you forward…pushing everything in front of you. Well, that's how I felt.

I walked to the back of the church. A crowd of men and women surrounded the man that God wanted to free. I felt the Lord wanted me to put my hand on his chest. It was pretty weird for me, but I was obedient and asked permission to touch his chest. He nodded yes. As soon as I touched him I had a very detailed vision. As I viewed it in my minds eye, I described it to the man. I saw a long hallway with many doors. The hallway had a bright light. Each door was shut. As the Lord revealed each thing (sin) that he needed to be freed from a door would fly open and the light from the hall would flood into the room. However, at the end of the hallway there was a door with many locks on it. I asked the man what was behind that door just as I had asked him about the others. He hung his head and couldn't bring himself to say it. The Lord made it clear to me that if he would repent of this secret sin, he would truly be free. I told him that he not only needed to open the door but he needed to break the locks on the door by confessing the sin out loud. I waited with my hand on his chest begging God to help him. It seemed like forever before he finally spoke it out. As soon as he did, the people standing around us crowded in. They were supporting, loving and hugging him. It was wonderful!

To be perfectly honest, if I had known the sin before that confrontation, I probably would not have had the courage to deal with it. I think sometimes it is easy to mistake unsanctified mercy for true mercy. Unsanctified mercy allows people to remain in bondage to sin out of some misplaced notion of love and grace. We don't want to make people (or ourselves) uncomfortable, so we gloss over sin. We make a way for sin. True mercy loves the person enough to be embarrassed or inconvenienced. It is willing to be misunderstood. It pursues the freedom promised by God which is complete and holy. True mercy does not shy away from the truth spoken in love.

I believe the Lord wanted this man to know the level of love and acceptance He had for him through his friends that crowded around him. All of them knew the sin that held him in bondage. I didn't know, but God used me to bring it into the light so he could be free.

This confrontation opened up a time of intercession for this man that lasted about a year. The Lord taught me many things through that experience. One of those things was when I had a major flare up of lupus while I was praying for him. I heard the threats of the enemy. It was clear this physical attack was directly from the enemy because I was praying for this man. I am ashamed to say that I wanted to stop praying for him. I told the Lord, 'He's not even my friend! Why should I lay my life on the line for him?' The Lord's response was, "He's my friend. And you are my friend if you do what I'm asking you to do." So with fear and my small faith, I reaffirmed my commitment to intercede for him and immediately the symptoms subsided.

John 15:13
**"Greater love has no one than this that one <u>lay down his life</u> for his friends**.

In this scripture, God is not only referring to <u>our</u> friends, but His. He asks us again to join Him in His intercession.

The Lord has allowed me to lead and be a member of several groups of people interceding for various people and it has been a great honor.

I think people who don't value intercession enough to actively participate in it are simply ignorant of how wonderful the benefits are. They may have never experienced the blessings of being connected with others for a like purpose and goal in prayer. Or they may not have been the subject of intercessory prayer themselves. That's why it is so important for those of us who have benefited, to continue to participate. We, by our involvement, can spread the news! When we intercede for people we are most like Christ…after all, <u>it was the job He was **Dying** to do…Now He **lives** to always intercede for us.</u>

## THE KEY OF TRUTH

I didn't know how to speak the truth in love. The Holy Spirit needed to teach me…and I needed to start listening and learning from Him.

Eph 4:15
but speaking the **truth in love**, we are to grow up in all aspects into Him, who is the head, even Christ,

Telling the truth has never really been a problem for me. <u>But telling it with **love** eluded me for most of my life</u>. I thought I was being loving by just speaking the truth. But I was often so harsh or blunt in my presentation that many people could not receive it. And now I know it was my fault.

> After years of delivering cruel truth, I finally heard the whisper.
> "If they can't receive it, why are you still talking?"

That's the question the Lord asked me one day. I thought about that continually for weeks. If the point of speaking the truth is freedom…but my presentation makes it impossible for them to hear the truth…they are then unable to be free. I needed to STOP TALKING!!! I needed to listen and learn how to bring life, not injury or death, through the truth.

John 8:31-32
31 Jesus therefore was saying to those Jews who had believed Him, "**If you abide in My word,** then you are truly disciples of Mine;
32 and **you shall know the truth, and the truth shall make you free**."

Jesus was never cruel with the truth. He was direct and brutally honest to the Pharisees, but never mean. His passion for the Father's will was motivated by love. I asked the Lord to help me keep the passion for His truth while embracing His love for His children.

I need to take a little detour here. My intention was never to be cruel with the truth, but without the love of God directing me, I ended up speaking truth so bluntly that it came out sounding mean. My love for the truth was much stronger than my love for His children. This is not balanced at all. Rom. 11:22 tells us that God is both kind and severe. Without love, the truth is only severe, which doesn't represent who Jesus really is. My intention was to see freedom in someone's life; but if a word can not be received because of a harsh delivery, then no freedom can occur. Intentions may be righteous but the effect is contradictory if the delivery is flawed.

The learning curve was long, as it always is with me. I was not easy to teach. During that period the Lord led me through a time of understanding. Understanding how my methods had hurt others. He allowed people to be cruel to me and I was not allowed to defend or even explain myself.

This was more painful than I had ever imagined. I often cried out to the Lord to protect or defend me. He did not. Broken, defenseless and frightened of people is what I became. Once, I tried to defend myself. I opened my mouth to say what I was dying to say and nothing came out. I learned to just shut up and take it.

Jer 1:9-10
9  Then the LORD stretched out His hand and touched my mouth, and the LORD said to me, "Behold, I have put My words in your mouth.
10  "See, I have appointed you this day over the nations and over the kingdoms, **to pluck up and to break down, to destroy and to overthrow, to build and to plant."**

Have you ever considered how the ground looks when a new building is about to be built? They cut down the trees, rip out the stumps, pull up every bush and dig a huge hole for the foundation. What about a field being turned into a garden? The whole thing is tilled, usually with a machine that literally tears up the ground. The ground must be voided of all the things that are in the way of progress. He wouldn't build His temple on land with no foundation. He wouldn't plant His seed among the thorns. Why was I surprised when my land had to be torn up first in preparation for the garden that the Lord wanted to plant?

The Lord took me through this process of 'plucking up, breaking down, destroying and overthrowing' my old ways to speaking truth. He let me suffer the same pain I caused in other people.

Now if the Lord gives me a difficult 'word' for someone I bear the pain of it first. He causes me to 'carry' it so I know the cost of speaking the truth in love. It is expensive! I do not do it lightly and I always ask the Lord if I can please just pray for the individual and be spared the speaking part.

I mentioned 'carrying' a word above so I'll explain what that means to me:

To carry a word is to pray for the person for whom God gave the word. To ask the Lord for His perfect will for that person. It is laboring in intercession with God for their good, which is standing in the gap between their present and the future to which the Lord is drawing them. Carrying a word for someone is to wait for the Lord's perfect timing so they will be blessed. It is a sacrifice that requires patience and the unselfish love of the

Father for His child.

By way of example, I once received a hard word for someone I loved. For days, I was hounded by the Lord.

Jer 23:29
"Is not My word like fire?" declares the LORD, "and **like a hammer which shatters a rock**?

Several times a day I heard the Lord say this scripture to me. At that point I was not aware that there was a scripture that said, "My word is like a hammer to shatter rock". That's what He kept saying. Finally I asked my husband if there was a scripture about God's word being a hammer. He said it was in Jeremiah. Oh boy…I had hoped I was making it up in my head. You know, like when you think you have a 'pizza' dream. If it's not a God thing, then you have no responsibility…but if it's from the Lord, you must search it out with Him. No word, dream, vision or teaching that comes from the Lord should be ignored. We are responsible for all that He gives us.

After I found the scripture, I asked the Lord what He was requiring of me. Then He put this person on my heart. I spent weeks weeping in prayer. I didn't even know why. But my heart was grieving for him. When that time of prayer had reached its fullness, (you never know how long the Lord will require you to pray and wait) He gave me the message I was to convey to that person. It was odd in a way because they (he and his family) had moved away a couple of years before. So I typed it out and sent it to them.

It was a warning and a rebuke. I was afraid to say or send it because I really loved that person. And I wanted them to love me too. I didn't want to lose him as a friend.

But the Lord had gone before me and softened his heart. He called me and repented in prayer that night. Later, I was told by other people who also moved there that they saw a big change in that person and wondered what I had said to him. I told them that it was not my place to share another person's word.

God is so smart, isn't He! He knows the timing and He knows the correct way of saying truth to bring about the best for His children. You're probably thinking, well of course He knows! But, if that is so obvious, why don't we wait for Him all of the time? Why do we often run ahead of Him? Why do we think that we should say something as soon as we hear it?

His word is like a hammer. But He wants to cover that 'hammer' in layers of velvet love. It breaks but it does not crush. The velvet is what makes it easier to receive. It is correct timing; prayer before, during and after; it is love. And love seeks to heal and restore, not crush.

I understand a little bit about the weight and the value of speaking the truth with LOVE. It truly is a treasure beyond my comprehension. And I pray that the people I wounded in the past are healed and restored to wholeness in His name.

## **THE KEY OF AWESOME SPIRITUAL WARFARE**

Have you ever noticed that before people get married the enemy does everything under the sun to get them to have sex? And after they're married, he does everything he can to separate them. Have you ever considered why that is?

Matt 18:19-20
19 "Again I say to you, that **if two of you agree on earth about anything that they may ask, it shall be done for them** by My Father who is in heaven.
20 "For **where two or three have gathered together** in My name, there **I am in their midst**."

Eccl 4:9-12
9 **Two are better than one** because they have a good return for their labor.
10 For if either of them falls, the one will lift up his companion. But woe to the one who falls when there is not another to lift him up.
11 Furthermore, if two lie down together they keep warm, but how can one be warm alone?
12 And if one can overpower him who is alone, two can resist him. **A cord of three strands is not quickly torn apart.**

So, if we are unified together, God is there and will answer our request and we can do more while protecting each other and keeping warm and secure in bonds that are difficult to destroy. Wow! No wonder the enemy wants to keep us apart.

In our marriage, the Lord put two people with dramatically different perspectives and methods together. My husband has the wisdom of a teaching/pastoring gift. He can see the journey ahead. He gets the road map, so to speak. I get a tiny piece of the puzzle. The Lord sometimes lets me see what's in the way of progress, or maybe the destination point. I might know why they can't get there or where they need to go, but I don't necessarily know how to get them there. In short, Wade knows the 'how' and I know the 'what'.

The team that God has made us to be is a great pleasure to us. And I believe that if there is a spirit of generosity in a marriage and a true appreciation for each other's gifts, God can do amazing things.

John 17:23
**I in them, and Thou in Me, that they may be <u>perfected in unity</u>**, that the world may know that Thou didst send Me, and didst love them, even as Thou didst love Me.

The NIV states that we may be brought to complete unity. Perfected, completed or fulfilled in unity with each other and the Lord.

Eph 4:3-6
3 being diligent to **preserve the <u>unity</u> of the Spirit** in the bond of peace.
4 There is **one** body and one Spirit, just as also you were called in **on** hope of your calling;
5 **one** Lord, **one** faith, **one** baptism,
6 **one** God and Father of all who is over all and through all and in all.

I realize that the **ONENESS** that these scriptures speak of is oneness with the Lord and the whole body of Christ. But how much more unified could two people in marriage be with each other and the Lord? One with Him and one with each other forming an almost indestructible cord of three banded together in His name. Being one in every way, mind, spirit and body. If you let yourself consider the miracle of being that connected, it takes your breath away.

Hang onto your hats! Frankly, great sex within a marriage is powerful spiritual warfare! By 'great sex' I mean both spouses experiencing satisfaction, not just one or the other. This subject matter may make some of you a little uncomfortable, but just consider what damage you could do to the enemy through your unity. And imagine what damage he can do to you, your family, as well as the church by dividing you or uniting you outside of God's grace. We must fight to keep that three-strand cord of the marriage and the Lord unbroken. We can not allow ourselves to be divided.

Now we see that the goal of spiritual warfare is to keep the unity in the bond of peace, as Eph 4:3 states. Before marriage, the preoccupation with sexual desire distracts us from His plan, which is a faithful union with our future spouse and Him. After marriage, problems associated with sex, usually not enough of it, distracts us away from the three strand unity that the Lord prefers for us.

Jesus' last recorded prayer before He was taken to suffer was that we be one. We should consider how to participate in His dream for our future.

John 17:20-22
20 "I do not ask in behalf of these alone, but <u>for those also who believe in Me through their word</u>;
21 **that they may all be one**; even as Thou, Father, art in Me, and I in Thee, that they also may be in Us; that the world may believe that Thou didst send Me.
22 "**And the glory which Thou hast given Me I have given to them; that they may be one, just as We are one;**

The Father, the Son and the Holy Spirit are ONE. You, your spouse and God are One....ACT LIKE IT!

## THE KEY OF SEEING THROUGH SOMEBODY ELSE'S EYES

I have mentioned before that I used to do some work in the arena of politics. At that time, I had two male bosses. They were/are both believers and men of integrity. I respect and admire them both to this day.

One night several months after I had stopped working for them, I had a dream. I dreamt they came to my house and I invited them in. They started to tell me that I could no longer work for them because they were aware of a sin in my life. They said that I could not represent them or their constituency because of this sin. Stunned, I asked about what in the world they were talking. They couldn't believe I didn't know to what they had referred. They said, 'Come on Gayle. We know that you're gay!' I protested vehemently, "It isn't true! Who told you that? Who is telling these lies about me?" They just shook their heads as they walked toward the door. I couldn't believe they wouldn't even listen to me. So as they left my house, I told them that if they didn't care enough about me to even hear me out, then they weren't my friends and maybe they never were.

When I woke up, I was sitting up, breathing hard and sweating. I was so agitated I could hardly breathe. I had to get up. I remained awake for the rest of that night pacing the floor. For weeks every time I saw one of those men, I was embarrassed and ashamed. I knew it was just a dream, but it left such a strong impression on me, I wasn't sure what to do. That feeling of being falsely accused and having no way to defend myself left me demoralized. It was so overwhelming and it wasn't even real.

Did the enemy send this dream? If he didn't, why would God send such a hurtful dream? It must be from the enemy, I thought.

Then about two years after the dream, the Lord drew me into a prayer ministry for homosexual people trying to come out of that lifestyle in obedience to the Lord. As soon as the opportunity arose, I remembered how ashamed, rejected, and judged I felt in that dream.

I know it wasn't real and that I didn't really experience that rejection. But the pain of how it felt to be so utterly dismissed and almost hated has never left me. It helped me understand a tiny bit of how painful that choice must be. **<u>No</u> sin weighs more than another (see I Cor. 6:9-11)**…all sin separates us from God…but the shame that the enemy loads onto someone in this bondage is so great. How could I not pray for them?

The Christian community can be so cruel to homosexuals. We are taught to hate the sin but love the sinner…since we all are sinners it shouldn't be that much of a stretch. But I have witnessed too often the judgment against these people and I am embarrassed by our lack of love. We are His kids…We have all fallen short. How dare we place more weight on one sin over another? Where is His love? Jesus didn't come in judgment. If He had, where would any of us be? We are all in need of a savior.

I just want to make sure that we are all on the same page about sin choices.

I Cor. 6:9-10
**9** Or do you not know that the unrighteous will not inherit the kingdom of God? Do not be deceived; neither fornicators, nor idolaters, nor adulterers, nor effeminate, nor homosexuals
10 nor thieves, nor *the* covetous, nor drunkards, nor revilers, nor swindlers, will inherit the kingdom of God.

In the I Cor. Scripture above, it says that all kinds of sinful behavior are not permitted if we want to enter the Kingdom of God. From sexual sin to theft, from being drunkards to being envious, **all** of these things are unrighteous and make us needy for a merciful Savior.

Micah 6:8
He has told you, O man, what is good; and what does the LORD require of you but to **do justice**, **to love <u>kindness (mercy)</u>**, and to walk humbly with your God?

Being involved in politics for conservative family values, I have witnessed Christians being very unloving, judgmental and even mean to gay people. NO SIN WEIGHS MORE THAN ANOTHER! How dare we, who are supposed to be Jesus to the world, be so hateful sometimes? It's unnecessarily cruel. We should check our hearts before we judge another…take the log out of our own eye first…….

We truly want to represent the Lord. His ways are higher than ours. It is the wisdom of God to stand for His justice in requiring truth and repentance. But it is also His nature to be kind and merciful. And to walk with the humility that understands there but for the grace of God…

## **THE KEY OF TEAM WORK**

This key is called 'Team Work', because God formed the team. He pulled us together from different backgrounds, perspectives and gifts. He united us for a purpose, which ultimately we were unable to accomplish. The Lord asked us to fight prayerfully for a miracle; a healed marriage. But as always, people must choose for themselves how they will live and what they will believe. One person cannot decide for two. And a team of people cannot decide for a couple. Still, we found the Lord in the process.

1 Cor 12:26-27
26 And if one member suffers, all the members suffer with it; if one member is honored, all the members rejoice with it.
27 Now **you are Christ's body, and individually members of it**.

One day I was hanging out with God, just talking. I had no pressing need. I wasn't worshipping, we were just hanging out together and He dropped a woman into my mind. She was an acquaintance I didn't know all that well. The Lord started speaking to me about her marriage. They were having a difficult time but I wasn't aware of much more. I moved on in my thoughts to something else and the Lord moved me back to her. It was a little puzzling because I was aware of whom her friends were and they are mighty prayer warriors, so I wondered why God wanted to enlist me into this particular battle.

He then gave me several names. Some were people that I already knew and some were people that I knew only by name. The Lord told me to bring them together as a team and lead them in intercession for this couple. I'm embarrassed to say that my response was to argue with God. I gave Him all the reasons that He should choose someone else to lead this team of intercessors.

1. I did not know all of them.
2. I was far less mature spiritually than many of them.
3. I didn't have experience leading an intercessory group at that time.
4. I didn't even know the couple that well, so they probably wouldn't trust me.
5. I didn't know if all of these people that God had given me knew the couple either.

## "Here I am, Lord…send someone else….PRETTY PLEASE!"

Being the person of faith that I am…I did what all people of faith and power do, I threw out a fleece! I had lots of faith, Huh? I told the Lord that I would know this was His idea if each person was excited to be involved and also volunteered the information about how they each knew this couple.

Well, that's exactly what happened. They all said yes almost instantly and started telling me stories about how they knew the couple. A few of the men even lived with the man in the couple about thirty years prior to this opportunity and were wondering how they were doing.

My next little faith hurdle was wondering why the couple's closest friends were not on the list. I tried to convince God to add them…but He didn't. I'm still not sure why. Maybe the couple needed someone to talk to that wasn't in the group. I really don't know.

We met once a month together to pray and offer insights that we had received in our individual prayer times. Some of the people were very prophetic. Some were supernaturally gifted intercessors. Some had words of knowledge and wisdom. We performed prophetic acts as directed by a few of the members of this team. One woman seemed to know when the Lord was directing one of us to speak…one woman knew vital information from the past…a few were the leaders when we went to the couple's house to pray. Most of us were attacked in various ways in specific areas that this couple battled. It was quite a learning experience. I wish that I could report a victory, but I can't; their marriage ended in divorce. Even though the success we sought was not attained, we were a part of an intercessory team of which God Himself was a member.

I wrestled with putting this story in the book, but that's life, I guess. Sometimes we give it all we have and still God's best doesn't come. We all have free will, we all must make choices, and we all must live with them.

1 Cor 3:5-7
5  What then is Apollos? And what is Paul? Servants through whom you believed, even as the Lord gave opportunity to each one.
6  I planted, Apollos watered, but **God was causing the growth**.

7 <u>So then neither the one who plants nor the one who waters is anything, but God who causes the growth.</u>

We came together as a team that God created. He moved our hearts to love that couple. We joined the Lord in His intercession for them…we chose to lay aside our lives for a time, hoping that our sacrifice would bring them life. We learned to form a team with people we didn't really know in obedience to the Lord. And even though that marriage was not restored, I believe the Lord not only knit our hearts together but also shared His heart with us.

## **<u>THE KEY OF PUZZLE PIECES</u>**

In 2003, three couples from the church we were attending at the time, including my husband and me, went to the Philippines to visit our missionaries. During that time I still had Lupus, so the sun and heat were a big problem for me. You see, people with Lupus are often allergic to the sun. The other two wives had, like me, never traveled outside of the U.S. and were likewise apprehensive. But we all felt led by the Lord to go. When we were there, the other people went on various missionary day trips to see the different outreaches while I stayed at the hotel. I spent my time praying and wondering why the Lord wanted me to come because I could have prayed at home. I was frustrated and was having a hard time not questioning my value on this trip.

The second day the Lord began to speak to me about puzzle pieces. On their own they can seem to have no value at all. They are not always in a box that would tell what puzzle they belong to. One piece is so random and useless. I began to wonder if God was talking to me at all…because the feelings of inadequacy I was struggling with seemed to come from the enemy. I felt like that random disconnected puzzle piece.

1 Cor 13:9-12
9   For **we know in part**, and we prophesy in part;
10  but when the perfect comes, the partial will be done away.
11  <u>When I was a child, I used to speak as a child, think as a child, reason as a child; when I became a man, I did away with childish things</u>.
10  For now we see in a mirror dimly, but then face to face; **now I know in part, but then I shall know fully** just as I also have been fully known.

The Lord interrupted my 'reasoning' with this scripture. He seemed to be saying, 'Gayle, just ask me about the puzzle pieces…don't try to figure it out without Me!' (You may have noticed that trying to figure things out without His help is a recurring problem I have)

So I asked Him. Then He began to give me small glimpses into the hearts of some of the people serving there in the Philippines. I wrote each thing down and prayed about them. I didn't know if I would ever say any of it because I wasn't even with them that much. So I prayed, I wrote, and I waited to see what God might do with His word. Maybe I was to keep a record of what God asked me to pray and give it to the leader of the ministry when we left. I didn't know what piece of the puzzle I was given. It wasn't up to me to figure it out.

A day did come when the Lord made a way for me to share what He had given to me for them. It was a pleasure to share. However, I think I learned more about keeping a confidence with God, which was a more valuable lesson for me personally.

Prov 25:2
It is the <u>glory of God to conceal a matter</u>, but the **<u>glory of kings is to search out a matter</u>**.

A consistent message I receive from the Lord is to **search things out**; to be my own king! To resist relinquishing the search for answers to someone else by asking other people what something means, instead of asking the Lord. He has also encouraged me many times to turn to Him, not others, for meaning and understanding. It's not bad to ask for help in the area of understanding, but I think that God likes it when we turn to Him first.

Jer. 15:19c
They for their part may turn to you,
But as for you, you must not turn to them

I think that He wants us to want Him and what He has in His hands. In other words, He wants us to press into Him for His truth, His presence and every blessing and insight we can get from Him. In short, to be 'greedy' for the things of God! I think it pleases Him when we search out a matter that He has hidden. He hides from us sometimes so that we will pursue

Him and what He alone knows.

We all have a piece of the puzzle. You may think that your piece is the whole puzzle. That's the way some people with a 'cause' treat others that don't have the same 'cause'. When I worked at the Right to Life office, that's how I treated other believers. I questioned their passion for God. After all, if they didn't care enough to protect the unborn...

Or you may feel that your puzzle piece is so small and insignificant as to not matter at all; putting so much emphasis on how other people might see you or the things that matter to you.

Both are exceedingly pride-full claims. When we take either position, the focus is on ourselves and how WE feel about OUR puzzle piece. Let's settle this now...It is God's puzzle. He will pass out the pieces as He chooses...IT'S NOT ABOUT US AND HOW WE FEEL ABOUT THE PUZZLE PIECE WE HAVE!

I probably could have been a little gentler, but that is basically what the Lord was saying to me on the trip. He may choose to use me in a way that I am comfortable with, or He may not. It wasn't about me and how I wanted to function. Bond-slaves don't choose how, when or where they will serve...they just serve. I have been purchased. It's not my choice... My Master will choose for me and for you...if He is your Lord.

The other day I was visiting my mom. She had just finished putting together a puzzle on the dining room table. I went over to examine it. I was standing on the other side of the table and I wanted a better view, so without thinking, I tried to move around the whole puzzle as though it were one piece. Well, that didn't work. It buckled and split and came apart in three places. Some of the pieces fell to the floor. I hurriedly picked them up and tried to reposition the puzzle. Again my efforts only made things worse. My mom just laughed and I sat down with her as we put the puzzle together again. She said it didn't matter because she was finished and was going to put it away anyway. But I know that she likes to enjoy the finished product for a little while at least.

It hit me that God must observe me with a smile and possibly a laugh when I try to 'reposition' my life at an angle that is seemingly better for me. It doesn't really matter since He knows the end from the beginning.

He knows that it is already finished according to His timeline. But I'm sure I have more times than not disturbed the process.

Wade and I are now members of a new church body. We don't know if or how the Lord may choose to use us. But we try to surrender daily to His direction…for His pleasure. We try to keep our hands off the puzzle while He is fitting the pieces together. It feels like we have sat unfinished for a long time….waiting… waiting.

If you don't know what piece of the puzzle He has placed in you…ask Him. In His time, He will tell you; just as we are confident that He will fit us into this new body; this new structure of living stones; the great mosaic of people called to His purposes as one in Him.

KEY summarization: Fighting the good fight is all about having Jesus' perspective of the battle field.

Rev. 4:1 After these things I looked, and behold, a door *standing* open in heaven, and the first voice which I had heard, like *the sound* of a trumpet speaking with me, said, "Come up here, and **I will show** you what must take place after these things."

In the previous verse God gives us an invitation to, 'COME UP HERE'.

He wants to give us His point of view; He wants to SHOW us His higher vision. Without His perspective we won't really know who we are battling. We get caught up in the circumstance and think our enemy is the person with whom we may be having trouble. Our enemy is never a person it is always the enemy of our souls. The devil tries to confuse the issues making us angry at someone and lose the point. We fight for the Lord and what He wants. And what He wants is for everyone to know how much He loves them…THAT'S THE GOOD NEWS. We are safe in Him and He wants everyone to know His love and mercy.

1Tim. 6:7
 I have fought the good fight, I have finished the course, I have kept the faith

I want Paul's testimony. We can all finish the course, keep the faith and fight the good fight.

## Section III

## **ATTITUDE ADJUSTMENTS NEEDED REGARDING OTHERS**

The Lord knows His children better than they know themselves.

As we go through various circumstances, we see other people through our own thought processes, our internal filter, if you will. We tend to measure other people with our yardstick instead of measuring all according to the Word of God and what He reveals to our spirit. It is easier to 'know' people after the flesh than to 'truly know' them by the spirit.

To know someone by the spirit is to allow the Lord to show us what His testimony is of someone. To be fully influenced by His view of their heart. Knowing people by the spirit is to let God shape our perspective. Personality or past actions, while important, are not the only measurement we need to 'know' someone's heart. We can't settle for knowing a book by its cover.

I have made that mistake far too often. People are complicated. They often do and say things because of insecurity. So, more often than we realize, they (we) can be misunderstood. This misunderstanding leads to poor counsel and hurt feelings, among other things. Much of the discouragement could be avoided if we would first consult the Lord and let His Spirit guide us.

I have included three examples of 'knowing' a person according to the spirit; one from the Old Testament, one from the New and one from Wade's and my life together. Maybe it will shed some light on what I'm trying to explain in this portion of the book.

1. David, Saul, Abigail and Nabal  I Samuel 25: 2-17

SAUL: Saul was King of Israel. David was fleeing and hiding from Saul. God had appointed David to be King, so to Saul, David was a usurper to the thrown. Saul did not 'know' David after the spirit. He only judged him as a threat. So he hunted David in order to kill him. Saul didn't care what God knew of David. He wanted to keep his position and in order to do that, David must die.

DAVID: David knew God's testimony of Saul. But he rightly understood that God would give David the kingdom in His perfect time. So he, though on the run, still honored Saul as King. David fled because Saul was afraid of him. David had chances to take Saul's life and begin His reign of the kingdom, but he chose to wait for the timing of the Lord. David's heart was committed to honoring the Lord and the King.

NABAL: Nabal was a worthless man. He had no wisdom and made a life of foolish choices. He refused to respect or honor David…looking ahead to who he would be someday. He regarded David as an outlaw fleeing justice. He only saw the outside…the obvious. David was in the company of outlaws so that is what he was to Nabal. Nabal didn't 'know' David by the spirit…Nabal didn't even 'know' himself.

ABIGAIL: Abigail was very wise. She 'knew' her husband inside and out. She judged his heart as foolish and she was right. She took the high road and saved his life by being generous in place of her husband. She even offered herself as a sacrifice to protect him and his household. She 'knew' David by the spirit. She knew that he was a man of wisdom and grace who would one day lead the country. Her wisdom saved the day and the future for herself as well as David's own heart.

I Samuel 25: 30-33
30 "And <u>when the LORD does for my lord according to all the good that He has spoken concerning you, and appoints you ruler over Israel,</u>
 31  this will not cause grief or a troubled heart to my lord, both by having shed blood without cause and by my lord having avenged himself. When the LORD deals well with my lord, then remember your maidservant."
**32**     Then David said to Abigail, "Blessed be the LORD God of Israel, who sent you this day to meet me,
33    and <u>blessed be your discernment,</u> and blessed be you, who have kept me this day from bloodshed and from avenging myself by my own hand

Knowing someone according to the Spirit is like seeing their future in the Lord. Realizing who He means them to be and doing all you can to bring God's will into being. Saul and Nabal focused on today. They had no vision but self preservation for the moment. David and Abigail adopted a higher and farther vision. They lived each day as a part of a greater future. They purposed to call into being that which did not exist…yet!

2. Saul/Paul and Ananias Acts 9:10-19

SAUL (before he became Paul) was a known persecutor of the church. He had the authority to imprison anyone who named the name of Jesus. Saul was a very dangerous man to any true believer. But the Lord revealed Himself to Saul on the road, blinded him and told him to wait for God's provision of healing and wisdom about what to do with his life.

ANANIAS was a faithful servant of the Lord. God spoke to him in a vision and told him to go pray for Saul's healing. Ananias was afraid. He 'knew' Saul according to the flesh…he knew that he was dangerous to every Christian. He questioned God's word to him. The Lord had to give Ananias His perspective of Saul. God had to convince Ananias that Saul would be a great benefit to the body of Christ before he would go and put his own life at risk to pray for him. The Lord allowed Ananias to 'know' Saul after the spirit. The Lord showed Ananias who God would make Saul. He even told him that Saul would suffer for the kingdom. I think God did that to help Ananias be more willing to take the risk of faith that He was asking him to take.

**10** Now there was a disciple at Damascus named Ananias; and the Lord said to him in a vision, "Ananias." And he said, "Here I am, Lord."
11 And the Lord *said* to him, "Get up and go to the street called Straight, and inquire at the house of Judas for a man from Tarsus named Saul, for he is praying,
12 and he has seen in a vision a man named Ananias come in and lay his hands on him, so that he might regain his sight."
13 But Ananias answered, <u>"Lord, I have heard from many about this man</u>, how much harm he did to Your saints at Jerusalem;
14 and here he has authority from the chief priests to bind all who call on Your name."
15 But the Lord said to him, <u>"Go, for he is a chosen instrument of Mine</u>, to bear My name before the Gentiles and kings and the sons of Israel;
16 for I will show him how much he must suffer for My name's sake."
17 So Ananias departed and entered the house, and after laying his hands on him said, "Brother Saul, the Lord Jesus, who appeared to you on the road by which you were coming, has sent me so that you may regain your sight and be filled with the Holy Spirit."
18 And immediately there fell from his eyes something like scales, and he

regained his sight, and he got up and was baptized;
19 and he took food and was strengthened.

The Lord trusted Ananias to hear His instruction about Saul and obey even though doing so put his life at risk. God gave him His perspective of Saul. The Lord showed Ananias that Saul would become Paul and with that name change, his character would change as well. Ananias trusted the Lord's word regarding Saul and obeyed.

3. My husband and I had been married about one and a half years when we decided to allow a woman to come to live with us. She was three years older than me and was having a hard time financially, so we wanted to help. She took up residence in our basement.

A problem began to develop because I mistakenly assumed that chronological age was the same as maturity. I assumed that since she was older than I, she would be wiser and more responsible. This was not the case.

She spent most of her days in our basement watching TV. She didn't pay rent, help with chores or look for employment. We provided everything that she needed.

It took eight months for me to get to my limit. When I reached it, I came unglued. I accused her of purposefully taking advantage and using us. I told her that if she didn't change dramatically in the next week, she would find her belongings on the front porch with the locks changed. I was livid! Further, I let her know that she had better be up and showered and out of our house by 9:00 every morning looking for a job if she had any hope of staying with us.

I then went into nervous energy mode! I started cleaning Wade's office. I was a ball of energy. As I worked I prayed and told the Lord that if He wanted her to stay, He'd better help her to be wise in how she responded to me. If she was rude, I was going to kick her out right then.

About a half hour later, she knocked on the door. I opened it and looked at her with a mixture of emotions. I was concerned for her and me.

She said, "Gayle, can I talk to you for a minute?" She had her hands behind her back as she waited for my reply. I said yes, but encouraged her to be careful. She brought her hand from behind her and in it was the cut cord of the TV. "It's a gift to you. I don't want it any more. You can have it. I didn't know that I had hurt you, I'm so sorry. Please forgive me. You will see a change in me. I won't let you down anymore."

That was true. The next morning as well as the rest of the mornings that week, she was up early, showered and out looking for a job. She had one by the next week and started paying rent as soon as she could.

Because of my faulty assumptions regarding maturity, I let things build up to overflowing. I'm the one that made things so difficult. She needed someone to care about her enough to be honest and not pretend that everything was fine when it wasn't. **Peace is not the absence of conflict; it is working through the conflict to a resolution.** I have seen more times than I can count that 'mercy' people get that wrong a lot of the time. I will define what I think a 'mercy' person is: They are people so motivated by mercy that their actions often excuse people of sin. I am sure that this is not their intention, but when you quickly move away from conflict in order to avoid a confrontation, sin is often pushed aside. A 'forgive and forget' policy is adopted, but without resolution the problem still exists no matter how hard we try to forget. The conflict bubbles and boils under the surface and is sure to rise up at the most inconvenient times. Just because there is no yelling doesn't mean that turmoil isn't happening. A false pretence that things are 'fine' is a lie and frankly it's cowardly.

Once I finally outlined the boundaries, she could be successful. She just needed a little truth and direction. And I needed to stop assuming that she was trying to hurt or manipulate me. I was looking at her through my filters, which were skewed. I used to always see the worst in people because I tended to be suspicious of them…always wondering what they 'really' wanted. I needed to learn to see with the eyes of the Father who loves His children enough to see what's inside of them and love them anyway.

The following keys are representative of God's attempts to show me a more excellent way.

1 Cor 12:31
But earnestly desire the greater gifts. And **I show you a still more excellent way**.

This more excellent way is to love with the purity of God. I have not mastered this, and I can't think of anyone that I personally know who has accomplished this lifestyle of pure love. But Jesus came because He really would rather die than live without us. He proved that at the cross.

Maybe if we let Him, the Lord will help us truly love and fully 'know' each other. If we let Him give us His perspective and help us to 'know' the heart of His other children maybe then these adjustments will happen more smoothly.

## THE KEY OF DISSONANCE

Jer 6:16-17
16 Thus says the LORD, "Stand by the ways and see and ask for the ancient paths, where the good way is, and walk in it; and you shall <u>find rest for your souls</u>. But they said, 'We will not walk in it '
17 "And I set watchmen over you, saying, **'Listen to the sound of the trumpet!' But they said, 'We will not listen.'**

During a counseling appointment I became aware that this particular woman would require a little more follow up than I had originally expected. I began to pray and ask the Lord how He wanted to accomplish His will for her.

He gave me a little vision. It was a triangle (the musical instrument). On one side the word 'melody' was written, on the other side 'harmony', and along the bottom 'dissonance'. The Lord told me each side represented a person that He revealed and what we would bring to this woman. I called the two women who were to bring the melody and harmony; and the Lord asked me to bring the dissonance. This was a problem for me because I didn't know what dissonance meant.

So I looked it up!

Dissonance: A discordant mingling of sounds; <u>discord</u>. **Music. A combination of tones regarded as displeasing and requiring resolution.** Harsh disagreement; incongruity; discord

Yippee!!! I get to bring the noise that people don't want to hear.

Let me start by being perfectly honest. It really bugs me when God asks me to say the hard things to people. I don't like having people be afraid to see me...I want to be liked just like anybody else. But He knows I'll do whatever He asks me to do. So, I guess that's why He asks...but honestly, I'm not wild about that particular assignment.

Back to the story: I called a friend who happens to be an amazing musician. I asked him to explain to me what he thought dissonance meant. He said it's usually heard in more complex pieces. For instance, orchestrated musical pieces often have dissonant points within them. The music could be a fair or even good piece without dissonance, but the dissonance, the part of the music that sets you on edge and is difficult to hear, makes the music rich and sumptuous. He also explained that when playing a dissonant chord, one must be careful to be on pitch. If the chord is flat or sharp, the whole piece falls apart completely.

Great, no pressure! So I waited on the Lord, listening for the word that this woman did not want to hear. When I brought my piece of the triangle to her, she already knew. God had previously told her, but she had rejected His word to her. In her spirit she had heard the song before; she just didn't want to sing along.

It seems to me God often does that. He sends someone to tell us what we already know but are sometimes unwilling to obey. More difficult 'words' are usually spoken to us in the whispers of God. He gently speaks direction to us. Sometimes He has to tell us many times...but if we harden our hearts, He will tell another to help us MOVE in that direction.

You might wonder why dissonant or difficult 'words' are important in our lives as Christians. Jesus told His disciples once unless they ate His body, they would not be His disciples. Now that was a hard message! Many people left Him that day. They couldn't stand to hear that chord. Their minds couldn't understand it, so they let His words fall to the ground. He turned to His apostles and asked them if they would leave too. Peter's response was the answer every true and faithful believer gives.

John 6:68-69
68 Simon Peter answered Him, "**Lord, to whom shall we go? You have**

**words of eternal life.**
69 "And we have believed and have come to know that You are the Holy One of God."

Sometimes the Lord allows difficult things to come into our lives. We don't always understand it or want to hear what He is saying to us. But if we choose to stay with Him and play, sing or just listen to the songs He gives us, we will be all the richer for it; even if the song has discord within it.

Once when I was going through some tough times, I wrote a note to a friend of mine who is an associate pastor and told him boldly: I DON'T GET IT!!!!

He called me and said, "Hey Gayle, I've got a great idea! Lets start a small group and invite everybody who 'doesn't get it' to join. But there's a problem with that...the group won't be small...because NOBODY GETS IT!" I realized whining about not getting it was a waste of time and energy. I was simply putting off learning to trust the Lord in that struggle.

Maintaining the belief that He is the Holy One and that He is Good helps us keep our heads and hearts aligned with Him. Peter was the only man that had the guts to answer Jesus. Peter was also the only man to walk on water. He embraced the dissonant chord and realized a little bit of his potential.

The Lord will probably give you the opportunity to hear a hard message. When He does, He'll ask you to decide if you are going to continue to walk with Him, if you will distance yourself from Him or simply walk away. Walking with Him means to trust and praise Him in the hardship. It is worshiping Him before the trial is over and embracing Him in the darkness of grief and sorrow. Walking away is hardening your heart while appearing to still be with Him, but not yielding your heart completely to Him. This is the choice that Judas made. He was still with the apostles, but his heart was far from them.

And possibly, the Lord may ask you to bring a dissonant 'chord' to someone. You will have to decide if you love the praise of men more than being obedient to God. Jeremiah was faced with that choice many times. He was constantly telling the people what they didn't want to hear. His whole life was about playing the tunes that most people didn't want to heed. After I realized that the Lord only requires me to bring the dissonant chord occasionally, it's easier to be faithful to Him. And I am even more grateful for the example that Jeremiah lived.

## THE KEY OF REAPING A BETTER CROP

Gal 6:7
Do not be deceived, God is not mocked; for **whatever a man sows, this he will also reap**.

John 15:16
"You did not choose Me, but I chose you, and appointed you, that you should go and **bear fruit**, and that **your fruit should remain**, that whatever you ask of the Father in My name, He may give to you.

I heard a teaching about planting and harvesting. I think it came from Morningstar Ministry. The point was, if you want to reap something you have to plant it first. Sounds simple, doesn't it? So if you want to see kindness coming through your life, you must first plant acts of kindness, generosity and blessing toward others. If you want to harvest forgiveness and graciousness from someone's garden, you must often sow love, patience and grace into their lives before you can expect to get that crop through them for the church or the world. And I don't mean in a manipulative way. Not an 'I'll be nice to you so you will be nice to me' sort of thing.

Let me explain. A while back I surveyed the 'field' of my own life and found it wanting. Reevaluation is something I do regularly regarding jobs, relationships and personal circumstances. I used to be very critical, judgmental, unforgiving, ungracious and lacking in compassion. In other words, my field was full of dandelions. Obviously, I was not a very 'safe' person, and tended to be a bit surly and unapproachable. In short, I was often so direct and blunt I scared people.

The Lord began to change my heart. He was doing the work secretly, but my outward life needed to be changed as well. He gradually helped me change my lifelong pattern...but still I continued to reap dandelions. They kept springing up even though I had stopped planting them. The process was long, lasting several years. It required a lot of weeding and weeding and weeding, with some more weeding before I could begin to see the other crop I had planted coming up and bearing fruit. Then the hard part became being a good gardener and maintaining the crop and increasing it. I'm trying to learn to keep the soil tilled and to allow the Lord to create a soft heart from a hard one. Now I can reap the better crop that the Lord established in my once fallow field.

Jer 4:3
For thus says the LORD to the men of Judah and to Jerusalem, "**Break up your fallow ground**, and do not sow among thorns.

Hosea 10:12
**Sow with a view to righteousness, reap in accordance with kindness**; break up your fallow ground, for it is time to seek the LORD until He comes to rain righteousness on you.

I'd like to apply this principle to others we know and love. Some people are prickly because of pain from the past. Since they are wounded they need patience and tender tilling, lots of encouragement, faithful watering and continuous fertilizing to help them see a better crop. I hope we all want a better crop. So I try to remember how long and difficult the process was of weeding my own soil before I complain about how long it seems to be taking someone else to realize his or her better crop.

We must remember the 'time factor'. The Lord will reproduce a better crop in His time. It takes a long time to break up the fallow ground. And even after the new crop is planted, it takes what seems like forever to see growth. I remember being discouraged that other people didn't notice all of the changes I was letting God do under the surface. My heart was changing, but it was happening inside. It takes years for others to see all of the effort we are making for a better harvest. We want to say, "Stop judging me by who I was!" But we can't expect people to see underground. The proof of real change is in the better crop that comes someday in the future. We are known by our harvest now, not tomorrow.

Gal 6:9
And **let us not lose heart in doing good, for in due time we shall reap** if
    we do not grow weary.

God wants to see a better crop coming through you and me even more than we want to see it! He is wise and has perfect timing…sometimes it's all about patience.

## PIZZA DREAM??? ( Not sure if this is a key or not)

Prov. 25:2
It is the glory of God to conceal a matter, but the glory of kings is to **search out a matter**.

You might be wondering why I would put this story in this book. If I'm not sure if it was from the Lord, what's the point? Well, that is the point! Sometimes it's hard to know if the Lord is warning you about something…or if you're just having 'pizza dreams'. 'Pizza dreams' are all the dreams that aren't truly from the Lord. All we can do is search things out as best we can. We may never know for sure…but even these dreams can change our hearts and draw us to the Lord. So, if that's all that these dreams do…that's pretty great!

I had a dream one night about a nursing home. There were about thirty elderly people who lived there with me. Yes, I was a resident but I was only about forty-five years old in the dream. I dressed like them; I ate what they ate; my room was just like their rooms; the staff was the same for all of us.

It puzzled me that I was in this nursing home since I didn't appear to need any special care or have any debilitating illness. Nevertheless, I was part of this community.

One day we were all in line to enter the pharmacy to get our weekly prescriptions. We entered by a large door that appeared to be a garage door. As we walked in, I noticed that this part of the building was like a large warehouse. The various drugs were in large receptacles. The receptacles were like the containers that hold bulk grains at big grocery stores. A nurse would hand the residents a list of their prescriptions and they were responsible to go to the containers and scoop out what they were prescribed for that week.

When it was my turn I got my list and proceeded to the bins of drugs. I watched those elderly people scoop out huge amounts of drugs and pour them into little baggies. I couldn't help but notice that the container labeled 'Heart Medicine' wasn't heart medicine at all. The pills in that container were laxatives. Immediately I ran to the staff doctor and informed him that the container had been mislabeled. I was very alarmed. However, the doctor didn't seem to care at all. He told me that the elderly often need laxatives and if they were correctly labeled, they might not take them. But if they were labeled 'Heart Medicine' they would make sure to take their laxatives.

I was stunned. "What about the people who actually have heart problems, doctor?" I asked. He told me not to worry about them. He said the laxatives wouldn't hurt them.

Incredulous, I started to run around and tell the people that the bins were mislabeled. I wanted them to know what the pills really were. I told them we needed a competent medical staff here. I tried to convince them that we should alert our families about the incompetent medical care we were receiving.

They all became very angry. But they weren't angry with the facility management or the doctors. They were angry with me!

The next day I became aware of a plot to kill me. (I know it's a really really weird dream!) So in the dream, I snuck out while everyone was asleep and escaped; the dream was over.

I was completely bewildered about what this could possibly mean. So, after praying about it for a week or so and receiving no direction, I asked a friend who is known for interpreting dreams.

She said, "Gayle, you're such a whistle blower! The Lord's probably just giving you a 'heads up' about some feathers you're ruffling ". Then she asked me what organizations I was involved with at that time. I told her.

I went home and prayed about it. Was the Lord trying to alert me to something that wasn't quite right? Honestly, I didn't know for sure. However, I did find out about some things that were strange in a certain organization. I did alert the people in charge. Nothing sinister happened but my perspective was definitely not welcome. I ended up leaving that place about a year later. To this day, I still hear whispers of corruption, and I'm glad to be released from my involvement there. Now I pray they will yield to the Lord as He expands their vision.

All we can do when confronted with disturbing images is search the matter out with the Lord. And sometimes we have to put things in the back of our minds until we have a clear direction. But I believe that it is always wise to go to Him in search of truth. Since He is the Living Truth…where else should we turn?

## **THE KEY OF BEING A KING MAKER**

Marriage is an investment that we make from the days leading up to the "I DO!" until death parts us. We decide if that investment reaps dividends for our children, our children's children, and us of course, or if that investment goes belly up!

Prov 14:1
> The **wise woman builds** her house, but the **foolish tears it down** with her own hands.

Within the first year of marriage, the Lord asked me a question. He wanted to know if I would be a 'King Maker'. He said words to the effect that I had the power to make my husband the richest man on earth or a pauper. It was up to me. In whatever decision I made, whether to build him up or tear him down, I could choose the life I would live. It would be either spiritually rich or impoverished.

When I witness women belittling their husbands or disrespecting them in public, it really irritates me. I guess I'm just too pragmatic to live that way. When a woman tears down her husband she destroys her own house. I'm sure that there is a better way to say what I'm about to say but "THAT'S JUST STUPID!" (Or foolish if you prefer)

You might be speculating that I couldn't possibly understand how difficult it is for you, that your husband is not loving or supportive. And that I was obviously blessed with an amazing husband, so what do I know?

Well, I was blessed with an incredible husband. I will openly admit that

I hit the jackpot when it comes to spouses. However, I will also tell you that Wade did not become 'Wade' without me. In other words, most people who know him would say he is a man of integrity, wisdom and in short, a really great man, but he wasn't always *this* great.

We learned together to see and honor the gifts of God in each other. Learning through time to set each other up for success and provide opportunities for each other to shine. I am absolutely amazed at his wisdom in finding and presenting a comprehensive picture to help people find their way through difficult circumstances. He in turn respects how the Lord might tell me the one thing that is missing; that undefined piece of the puzzle that pulls the picture together.

Whether you're a woman who has been disappointed for many years in your marriage or a new bride, making your husband a king is difficult to implement into your life. But I can tell you that if you will purpose to encourage and build him up, your efforts will not be in vain. He will rise up and bless you. He will honor you and make a way for you.

I have often advised our daughter when considering who she may marry, to choose someone that she can continue to respect forever. Don't just think about the mushy feelings that are there now. Assess why he is an honorable man. Evaluate why he is worthy of your ever-growing respect. Because, according to the Word of God, respecting your husband is a big part of your job description as a wife.

I sent a rough draft of this 'key' to our daughter, Maranda. I talked with her after she had read it and she asked me where the rest of it was. I said, 'What do you mean?' She told me that what she read was only about half of what I had told her. 'Mom, you should give examples about how you made dad a king!' She said that since she would be married soon, she wanted to know what good things would come of being a king maker. I hesitated because I don't want her to manipulate her husband. But I also want her to have a successful marriage.

The examples that I can offer seem kind of silly because they are really just common sense. However, I have often witnessed married people doing the opposite, so maybe these simple suggestions are needed. Once again I must acknowledge that common sense isn't always common.

Examples:

1. Make your husband feel safe discussing his dreams and encourage him. It doesn't matter if you can imagine them being accomplished. They may be too big for you…but help your husband by believing in **him**. Even if he doesn't accomplish these exact dreams, he will be encouraged by you and be a better man.

2. HELP him! That's what we're called to do…help our husbands. Make a way for him to succeed by giving him what he needs. Time, encouragement, opportunity (by not saying NO when he asks), and serve him as he reaches for his goals.

3. Pray for him. Not in a manipulative way (Dear God, make my husband…). Pray that he realizes his value to the kingdom, family and you.

4. Don't withhold anything good that you have the power to give your husband. The thing that I have witnessed women withhold most often is sex. Don't do that...It's wrong!!!

These are just a few examples of how to build up the man God gave you. If you are like my daughter you may be wondering what the benefits are for you. Let me list some of what Wade has done for me in response.

Benefits:

1. He truly lays down his life for me. He takes care of my needs and me and never makes a decision without considering me or without my involvement.

2. On the frequent instances of physical pain I have dealt with, he has remained by my side. Often crying and pleading for mercy for me until that awful time has passed. He has served me more times than I can count and remained faithful to me when many lesser men would not have.

3. It is because of him that I have the courage to obey the Lord in writing this book. No one on this earth loves and encourages me

more. In making him a king…I have made myself rich!

When we have talked to young people about getting married we often ask the man what he thinks laying down his life for his wife really means. More understanding is always needed. But mainly I just point to my own husband. If I were to list all of the ways that he dies daily for me, it would take up too much space. I am not an easy person to live with! I have been sick for most of our marriage, which meant that normal things often went undone. He has had to do and sacrifice more than the average man sacrifices. And he never makes me feel bad about it. He just continues to love me in every way and I continue to feel overwhelmingly blessed.

I have just described how wonderful it can be. We still have trials but we meet them as ONE. Maybe your marriage isn't quite so wonderful. Maybe your husband has not always sacrificed so freely or you have not always built him up with abundant respect. There is a remedy! If you are convicted, repent. Stop tearing down your husband, your house. Instead, build him up into the man of God he is called to be. It takes no prophetic ability to see sin and fault, and to constantly point them out. But it takes great wisdom and prophetic insight to see what God has prepared for your spouse, to see him as God sees him. And with God's help, look past the faults we all observe as a result of living with someone in close proximity. By faith you must call into being that which does not exist and stand by his side until it is accomplished.

Rom 4:17
(as it is written, "A father of many nations have I made you") in the sight of Him whom he believed, even **God, who gives life to the dead and calls into being that which does not exist**.

Call forth God's vision for you together. Then you will eat the fruit of plenty in your marriage. You will begin to witness his dying for you. It's a humbling sight. It will break your heart for him and cause you to thank the Lord for bringing him into your life. God can still make you ONE. It is not too late to build your own house.

Now He is asking you, "Will you be a King Maker?"

Gayle M. Nelson

## **THE KEY OF EATING THE SCROLL**

Ezek 3:1-3
1  Then He said to me, "Son of man, eat what you find; **eat this scroll**, and go, speak to the house of Israel."
2  So I opened my mouth, and He fed me this scroll.
3  And He said to me, "Son of man, feed your stomach, and **fill your body with this scroll which I am giving you**." Then I ate it, and it was sweet as honey in my mouth.

We've all heard preachers expound on the wonders of God. But sometimes even though what they say is amazing, it can be completely powerless. I have come to believe that this happens when the one expounding has failed to first 'eat the scroll'. If it isn't REAL in their life, it won't be life changing for you or me.

How can His Sword be thrust with the power and passion of God when He was not first invited to wield it in our own life? How can it cut through another person's hard heart when it has not first sliced ours?

 This is how we eat the scroll: We allow the Lord to wield His sword within us. Cutting through every faithless hindrance we put in His way, we take His word into our hearts, minds and our very lives…we choose to live it.

Let me give a simple example:

Ps 118:24
This is the day which the LORD has made; let us rejoice and be glad in it.

We can and do sing this song with abandon. But, when the doctor tells you that you might die, or when someone you thought could be trusted – can't, or when your greatest dreams seem to fade until life becomes sadder and sadder and hope seems to evaporate…Is your testimony, "This is the day that the Lord has made!  I WILL REJOICE AND BE GLAD!"

Ezekiel said that the scroll tasted like honey. I guess what is difficult to bear can be sweet to remember.

If we choose to extract the precious from the worthless and eat the scroll before we try to serve it to others, and before we **claim** to be a spokesman for God, maybe that's when we get to taste the honey.

## THE WEIGHT OF FALSE EXPECTATIONS

Heb 13:21
equip you in every good thing **to do His will**, working in us that which is pleasing in **His** sight, through Jesus Christ, to whom be the glory forever and ever. Amen.

If we can occupy ourselves with **doing His will,** as mentioned in the previous scripture, we will be better able to stand against the temptation to be man-pleasers. When we are more concerned with pleasing others, we tend to manipulate them instead of finding our fulfillment in doing the will of God.

A couple from our previous church had left to go to another church. They returned several years later. Then they left again after a few years to plant another church. They are amazing people, and they are also our friends. They are mature and very gifted. Each time they returned, they came back even more seasoned with wisdom and experience than the time before. The Lord has given them a powerful testimony that everyone who knows them appreciates.

The time before they left for the last time (to begin a church in another state) was very rich. The man had gleaned wisdom in leadership and pastoring skills. And the woman carried herself with a stately grace. It was easy to honor them and all they had accomplished together.

One Sunday night, they came to Wade and I and asked us to pray for them. We asked if there was anything in particular that they needed prayer for. They said that there wasn't…they just wanted prayer. As we prayed I saw a picture in my minds eye. It is as follows:

I saw a beautiful, lush tree. It was a deciduous fruit tree with lots of foliage. As I examined the tree, I noticed that I couldn't see the fruit. I also observed that the branches were so weighted down with leaves that they appeared to be starting to break under that load.

I was puzzled at the sight of the tree, so I asked the Lord what He was trying to tell us. I felt He wanted me to ask them if they were overwhelmed with the weight of other's expectations on them. When I asked, tears filled their eyes as they began to explain how overwhelmed they were. It was a weight they could not and should not have to bear. We began to pray for release for them when the Lord showed me that I was guilty of loading them up with my own false expectations.

When I realized that I, their friend, was one of the people who was making life so difficult, it broke me. I started to cry. I then confessed to them that I was one of the people that had weighted them down with my expectations; things that had nothing to do with the calling the Lord had for their lives. These expectations were just foliage on the tree that needed to be pruned away so the fruit could come to maturity. Human expectations robbed them for a while of the freedom to live the life that God had set before them. I asked for forgiveness and they graciously gave it to me.

When we pile expectations on people, we distract them from that which God is calling them. Godly people often want to make others happy. So when we load them up with pressures to make us happy, God's desires for them can get sidelined. People can refuse to be manipulated…but few are strong enough (at least at first) to stand up to that kind of pressure.

I didn't mean to hurt them or cause them any grief. But I think it is all too easy to do this type of thing to others. Here are a few ways that we commonly heap on the weight of false expectations:

1. We ask someone for a favor. But we aren't really asking. We expect them to do it.

2. Sometimes we ask if we are interrupting, as though that would stop us from continuing…but we don't expect people to say, "Yes. You have interrupted me!" We expect them to stop whatever they are doing to hear or help us.

3. We ask for honesty, while really just wanting them to tell us what we want to hear.

4. We even ask people to pray, expecting that they will only give a word from the Lord that will tickle our ears. We expect a 'pleas-

ant' word...not a true word from the Lord...no matter what He may say through them.

5. We expect easy relationships that cost nothing and are worth even less.

When I ponder that vision the Lord gave me for my friends, I'm grateful for His patience with me. He is kind to show me the truth about my heart...how selfish I can be. My friends needed to be released from all the selfish expectations on them so that they could be what God designed them to be for His sake.

I'm determined to try to remember not to do that to anyone else. But even if I do...there is always repentance and forgiveness. I hope to learn better ways to bless others so that they can realize the call of God on their lives. He is good and His grace is enough.

## THE KEY OF GETTING IN THE GAME

2 Tim 4:7
I have fought the good fight, I have finished the course, **I have kept the faith**;

One of the things the Lord changed my mind about totally changed my life. I became free in an area that had long plagued me with disappointment and hopelessness. I saw our daughter believing the same lie, and more than anything I wanted her to be free as well. So I talked to her about this mind change. In fact, I started to nag her. I didn't mean to be a nag, but I was. One day we were talking on the phone and she basically told me to 'back off'. My nagging was causing her to dig her heels in and resist my suggestions.

So, I started praying to the Lord in my heart. "Oh God, give me some story or analogy to help her see the freedom that awaits her. Please help me to whet her appetite for this revelation." His response to my request was to give me a football analogy.

I couldn't believe it! "God, give me a break! I hate football and so does she (at that time in her life). Give me something else." He met my request with SILENCE. So I told her the analogy.

"OK Maranda. It's as though you're at a football game." I heard her groan. "And you go to these games every chance you get. You have the giant foam finger, you do the wave with the crowd, and you practically lose your voice at every game cheering your team to victory. You are a faithful, fervent fan. But you are not a player, and you don't even think that you can be one."

"It's time to suit up and get in the game! Catch a pass, make a touchdown, tackle somebody and take a risk of being tackled. Maybe the other team will get some yardage on you. They may even seem to be winning at times. But we will be the season's champions. Victory is within your grasp. Find out your position and play it with all you've got. There is a place for you on the team. But you've got to get out of the stands and get in the game. "

I sat silently waiting for her response, all the while knowing that it was a ridiculous analogy for a girl that never even went to a football game in school. The silence was broken, "Mom, everything that you have said before really annoyed me. And I couldn't hear what you were saying because you were bugging me so much. But, what you just said made more sense to me than anything else. I'm ready to do what you've been asking me to do."

God's so smart! He knows the key and He knows how to turn it so we can walk through the door to freedom and step into His promises. Prophetic promises are usually conditional. We must participate in the fulfillment of His word. Participating with Him in His vision for our lives is what getting in the game is all about.

God may have spoken a word of faith to you about your future. But it is not solely up to Him to cause it to come to pass. This book for instance. I have been prophesied to regarding writing a book. For years I was clueless about what the Lord wanted me to write about. In fact, I ignored most of those prophecies. Then the Lord directly prompted me to write it. It was not up to Him to write it, edit it or make adjustments and corrections. It was not up the Lord to publish it. If I continued to be unwilling to follow through, you would not be reading this book right now. And even worse, I would not have been changed in the process. I would have missed out.

I needed to be a player on my own team in obedience to the Lord. I am in the game!

I mentioned this little story to a friend. She told me that the Lord had promised her something a few years ago. She has been waiting for Him to bring it to pass. When she heard the story she was immediately convicted that she had a part to play. Passively waiting for something instead of fighting aggressively in prayer and faith (living it before it comes to pass) is unproductive at best. She's getting in the game now!

1 Tim 1:18-19
18 This command I entrust to you, Timothy, my son, **in accordance with the prophecies previously made concerning you, that by them you may fight the good fight**,
19 keeping faith and a good conscience, which some have rejected and suffered shipwreck in regard to their faith.

C. S. Lewis said, "Only real risk tests the reality of a belief."

It's risky to take God at His word; to believe and confess His truth before the evidence is presented. Risky when the other team enjoys not only tackling but killing, stealing and destroying. But we can't just show up and expect God to play the game without any other players. We've gotta' get in the game!

## THE KEY OF A WHIRLWIND / TWISTER / STORM

Rom 2:3-4
3 And do you suppose this, O man, when you pass judgment upon those who practice such things and do the same yourself, that you will escape the judgment of God?
4 Or do you think lightly of the riches of His kindness and forbearance and patience, not knowing that the **kindness of God leads you to repentance**?

During one of my hospital stays, the elders of our church came to pray for me. Before they came, all I could do was lie in bed and listen to music, pray or sleep. Since I was grateful they were coming I asked the Lord to give me some way to bless them. Falling in and out of sleep…I dreamed.

I dreamt that they (the elders) were at an airport. They were all standing just inside a huge airplane hanger. The giant doors in the front of the hanger were open. As they stood there looking outside, a twister or whirlwind appeared directly in front of them. It was so large that from inside the hanger they couldn't see how large it was since it filled (blocked) the entire opening.

As I watched them, the Lord caused me to understand a few things.
1. They were afraid.
2. They knew that they were to enter into the whirlwind (the storm)
3. The twister (storm) represented someone in the church.
4. Some damage would come from this whirlwind (storm).
5. The damage was unavoidable.
6. They would be responsible to do the clean up.

I told them the name of the person I thought was in the center of the storm. There was some agreement but no understanding.

Several years later the whirlwind came in the form of a secret sin that was revealed. This sin had taken place many years prior to its exposure to the elders. News of it was very devastating to the body. Many people were disillusioned and could not get past the feelings of betrayal and loss. Disagreements about how to 'handle' the situation (storm) were countless.

The saddest thing about it to me is that it all could have been avoided. This sin would have been thrown into the sea of forgetfulness if the humility of repentance had come first. The only one who would have known would have been the accuser of the brethren (Devil) and grace would have covered it.

The lack of repentance is the predominate reason we must go through the whirlwind. The arrogance in refusing to repent, as though it was an unusual state in Christendom, brings the storm. The whirlwind is God's gracious reminder that we are lost in sin without Him. In neglecting to repent we are asking for the inclement weather. Repentance must be our life style. It is and should always be common within the church.

I believe that when we repent the Lord actually forgets our sin against Him. We are free from judgment and shame. But we must acknowledge our own sin and humble ourselves before Him and receive His grace to come clean.

Amos 3:6
If a trumpet is blown in a city will not the people tremble? If a **calamity occurs in a city has not the LORD done it?**

I know that Amos is not a 'happy' book to get a scripture from, but the above verse describes what happens when we resist the Lord and choose to remain hard hearted. The sin we commit against God brings hardship of its own. But the lack of repentance brings the merciful hand of God to bear. Calamity doesn't sound very merciful does it? But if the fruit of public exposure is an unveiled face looking at the Lord in repentance and being transformed into His likeness…What enormous mercy it is!

2 Cor 3:17-18
17 Now the Lord is the Spirit; and **where the Spirit of the Lord is, there is liberty**.
18 But we all, with <u>**unveiled face**</u> **beholding as in a mirror the glory of the Lord, are being <u>transformed into the same image</u> from glory to glory**, just as from the Lord, the Spirit.

During the process of walking this person through repentance, and all that it entails, I saw a vision. I actually saw the elders in the same airplane hanger I had seen in that dream so many years before. The whirlwind was raging as before but they were entering into it now. The extremities, the top, bottom and the swirling sides were filled with all kinds of debris. To be anywhere inside the whirlwind other than the center was extremely hazardous. It was critical that they remained in the center of the storm. If they tried to escape before the danger had subsided many would be lost.

As I remember those difficult days, I must admit that I wanted to escape before the Lord was finished. It was a painful time. The conclusion wasn't all that I hoped it would be, but I'm glad we stayed in the middle and rode that storm out. The Lord paid the price for our sin. All we are required to do is acknowledge that through repentance. If we don't humble ourselves, we will reap the whirlwind.

KEY summarization: Adjustments in thinking rightly about others are achieved by being willing to see how the Father sees. He sees what is in the heart. Truth and love direct his movements. If we will let Him, we can have His vision and love others with His love.

## Section IV

## **LESSONS THAT ARE BIGGER THAN ME**

Since all of the 'keys' in this book have some reference to the Lord and how amazing He is,
I suppose every 'key' could fall into this category. His ways are so much higher and bigger than mine.

When I think of concepts like Mercy, Repentance and the Timing of God, I am troubled with my lack of understanding…These monumental ideas from the very heart of God that we distill into one-word descriptions are obviously beyond me. Admittedly, I'm in over my head. I honestly can't claim to bring any more understanding than what you probably already possess, but I have been urged by the Lord to write what He has shown me, nonetheless.

So, the following keys are the Lord's instruction to me regarding my own personal learning curve of the following things that are too big for me. The lessons are not complete, but it's a beginning; like a small window pane of a dark house that has been cleaned so some of His light can shine through. I hope a little bit of His light is better than none.

## **THE KEY OF GETTING OUT OF JAIL**

Repentance is your 'Get Out of Jail FREE" card. This 'key' is about living a lifestyle of repentance. We all have repented at least once when we came to the Lord. But I believe the closer we get to Him, the more we see Him for who He really is. That vision of His majesty and holiness is a measurement of which we fall far short. Seeing the truth of His greatness against our humanness causes our hearts to realize our urgent need and deficiency. We just don't measure up. That fact does not escape His notice, so He has provided a <u>remedy: Repentance</u>.

A friend of mine used to say, "Get low (humble) and stay low (humility)". This was his way of saying that if we see ourselves accurately, we will be more inclined to live a repentant life. I think he was right.

Gal 5:1
<u>It was for freedom that Christ set us **free**; therefore keep standing firm and do not be subject again to a yoke of **slavery**.</u>

Rom 8:15
For you have **not received a spirit of** <u>slavery</u> **leading to fear** again, but you have received a spirit of adoption as sons by which we cry out, "Abba! Father!"

Sometimes the Lord puts someone on our hearts. We think about them so much that we begin to pray for them and seek the Lord for their well being. And sometimes the Lord leads us to get involved in their lives directly. This happened with a woman I barely knew…which is often how I've gotten to know people; first by His spirit, then by a natural relationship. Anyway, the Lord revealed to me an area of sin bondage in her life. I was compelled to walk with her for as long as the Lord directed; encouraging and helping her in any way that I could for His sake. This lifestyle of sinful behavior had permeated her life and she seemed trapped in it. I asked the Lord how I could help her. The following is a vision He gave me for her and anyone trapped by sin.

I saw a tiger cage. It was huge and had steel bars on the top and all around the sides with a wood bottom. In the corner of the cage was a twin bed with a pretty comforter and pillow shams. Around the cage were picture frames hung by 'S' hooks from the cross bars, and a colorful fluffy circular rug lay on the bottom. The woman was sitting on the bed relaxing. I also observed that the cage door was ajar. She looked up and saw me and motioned for me to enter into the cage and make myself comfortable. I refused, knowing somehow that I was not to enter but to try to help her leave her cage.

I sought the Lord about what the vision meant and what I was to do with it. Should I remain silent and keep praying or should I also tell her what the Lord was showing me.

The next time that we met the Lord gave me permission to tell her the vision and what it meant. The Lord showed me that she had made a jail for herself. She had entered into a lifestyle of sinful behavior that she was unwilling to resist. And instead of leaving it she had made it comfortable to remain in bondage there. She wanted others to join her in this bondage and enjoyed the sympathy that others gave her as they viewed her in her cage. She liked looking between the bars and seeing the sympathy from others. The constant attention was like a drug to her.

I began (as compassionately as I could) to show her the way of escape: REPENTANCE! Ultimately she decided to stay within the jail that she had constructed for herself, choosing to be comforted by excuses and the attention of others, instead of the freedom that comes with repentance.

I watched several of her friends comforting her regarding this sinful life. They were angry with me because I seemed hard and unfeeling to them. As I watched our mutual friends, I was puzzled by their acceptance of her choices. They said they loved her as Christ would. But I disagree. Jesus never made people feel comfortable in sin. He loved and accepted them while at the same time, leading them through the door to freedom. He pointed out the sin of the woman at the well, but He didn't leave her there. He provided a way of escape. His loving truth released her and many in her community.

I remember that time with great sadness and a warning in my mind and heart. How easily we can deceive ourselves into thinking that there is no freedom. <u>How willing we are to settle for sympathy instead of healing and liberty; choosing as an alternative to act the victim.</u> How blind we can be not to see that the door is ajar and further, that Jesus made a way for freedom by His death in our place.

A few days after she made her choice to remain in bondage to this sin or jail, the Lord brought me another 'picture'. I saw hundreds of tiger cages in a huge pile. They were broken and piled up haphazardly. I felt that the Lord was telling me many would choose to leave their cage…their jail. And I should not loose heart. Many believers choose daily to be free and repent before the Lord. So, I continue to hope while presenting the key that we all should practice turning. The key of repentance that releases us from the jail we create through our choices to sin against God.

## **THE KEY OF THE TRUE POWER OF MERCY**

2 Cor 3:16-4:2
16 but **whenever a man <u>turns</u> to the Lord, the veil is taken away**. (*turn often means repentance*)
17 Now the Lord is the Spirit; and where the Spirit of the Lord is, there is liberty.
18 But we all, with unveiled face beholding as in a mirror the glory of the Lord, are being
transformed into the same image from glory to glory, just as from the Lord, the Spirit.
CHAPTER 4
1 Therefore, since we have this ministry, as **we received mercy**, we do not lose heart,
2 but we have <u>renounced the things hidden because of shame</u>, not walking in craftiness or adulterating the word of God, but by the manifestation of truth commending ourselves to every man's conscience in the sight of God.

When I was a baby Christian, I attended a women's bible study. One evening the teacher handed out a little test to all of us. She asked us to read each statement and mark the one that best fit what we believed. It was a gift test and each statement correlated to a spiritual gift. The first statement on the page read something like, 'The truth is the most important thing'. I read that first statement marked it and handed it in. It took me about ten seconds. The teacher looked at me and said, "Gayle, go back and read every statement before you answer." I went back to my seat thinking that it was a waste of time but that I might as well obey, thinking it would only take a few more seconds. I read them all and recognized that other things were important but they were not the MOST important, at least not to me. The last statement on the page was about the value of the mercy of God. I marked it and crossed out the first one. Then I changed my mind and crossed out the last one and re-marked the first one. I changed my mind several times and finally when everyone else had handed their papers in, the teacher asked me for mine. I ended up with the first one about truth being my final choice. But I realized that my motivation for valuing the truth so highly is born out of mercy.

Most of the people who know me probably wouldn't describe me as a 'mercy person'. Descriptors like, direct and 'in your face' have been used when referring to me. But **the reason I love the truth so much is because JESUS the person of TRUTH sets us free**. The Living Truth brings freedom to each of us. WOW! And the mercy of God won't allow me to passively watch people I love remain in jail. It's heart breaking. And I know when I am unwilling to tell them what the truth of God is, that's when I am lacking a loving mercy for them. True mercy will turn the key by praying and/or saying what some may not want to hear. True mercy will walk with someone through the process of repentance and risk rejection or being misunderstood by others to bring him or her through. Truth without mercy and mercy without truth are counterfeits of the real deal. True mercy brings hope and freedom; it is not sympathetic to bondage. When we embrace the person of Truth, we will not have mercy for anything under His judgment; which is unsanctified mercy. The key of mercy unlocks the jail cell and sets people free!

When we choose to be sympathetic to others and make excuses for sin, we are being selfish and cruel…not kind. The kindness of the Lord ALWAYS leads to repentance. If we choose to make others comfortable in their sin, we just want to be well thought of and liked above the desires of the Lord for that person. We are preferring to please men rather than God. True mercy puts the Lord and His will first.

## THE KEY OF EXTRACTING THE PRECIOUS FROM THE WORTHLESS

In the late 80's or early 90's, I was one of many spokeswomen for Right to Life in our state. We were running a ballot measure. If it passed the new law would require that parents be informed before their minor daughter could obtain an abortion.

I was somewhat familiar with public speaking, but not really in a formal political role. During that time period I had the opportunity to speak at schools, news interviews, and even one press conference (which I wasn't supposed to have to speak at…but ended up doing it anyway…long story).

For one of those speaking engagements, I was woefully unprepared. It was at one of the largest, most liberal high schools in our *progressive* city. My opponent was a former legislator who was a practiced and polished public speaker. I was not greeted warmly. After all, I was promoting a ballot measure that would ensure that their parents knew what many did not want their parents to know. In their minds, I was messing everything up! A real 'buzz kill'! I (being the only visible target that they knew) was going to make sure that their parents not only knew they were having sex, but when they got pregnant or when they impregnated someone. Advocating for Parental Notification was a very unpopular position, particularly at a high school.

Having done the best I could to bring out all of the pertinent facts, still I was clearly the loser at that event. A handful of students came up to the stage after the 'slaughter' and thanked me for coming 'anyway'. They also apologized for the heckling, swearing, and threats that I had endured. "Don't give up on us…there's still a few conservatives left here", they assured me.

As I walked out to my car, I started to shake. I got in and was almost hyperventilating. Having never reacted this way before, I was alarmed, to say the least. Driving home I vowed in my heart never to put myself through that again!

There was a message on my phone when I returned home. It said, "Thanks Gayle for being willing to go to *blank* High School tomorrow. I really appreciate it!" Then I remembered I had made that promise. How could I have been so stupid? This school was almost as bad as the one I had just come from.

The next morning I woke up and started getting ready. But the closer I got to the time I would have to leave, the more terrified I became. I had never experienced anything like it. Sure, I got nervous before speaking but this was ridiculous. I was shaking again. And I almost never shake! I know it is common for people to get nervous before public speaking engagements, but this was crazy! I was going to cancel but then I decided to call my church instead. The administrator was an excellent public speaker and had quite a bit of experience politically. He said he understood and asked me to close my eyes and listen as he read a scripture to me. He read the following.

Jer 15:16-21
16 Thy words were found and I ate them, and Thy words became for me a joy and the delight of my heart; for I have been called by Thy name, O

LORD God of hosts.
17 I did not sit in the circle of merrymakers, nor did I exult. Because of Thy hand upon me I sat alone, for Thou didst fill me with indignation.
18 Why has my pain been perpetual and my wound incurable, refusing to be healed? **Wilt Thou indeed be to me like a deceptive stream with water that is unreliable?**
**19 Therefore, thus says the LORD, "<u>If you return, then I will restore you</u>-- Before Me you will stand; and <u>if you extract the precious from the worthless, you will become My spokesman</u>**. They for their part may turn to you, but as for you, you must not turn to them.
20 "<u>Then I will make you to this people a fortified wall of bronze; and though they fight against you, they will not prevail over you; for I am with you to save you and deliver you,</u>" declares the LORD.
21 "So I will deliver you from the hand of the wicked, and I will redeem you from the grasp of the violent."

After he read this scripture to me, he prayed that the Lord would give me courage to speak for Him and for those who have no voice. I repented for fearing the enemy more than trusting God. Then peace flooded through me and I can honestly say that particular speaking engagement went very well.

Ever since that time, this has been a pivotal scripture in my life. When I get faithless and whiny about my life or some difficulty that seems unfair, I can hear the Lord say, "<u>If you return (repent), then I will restore you…</u>". Jer.15: 19 in particular is part of my DNA.

If you'll notice, the Lord did not spend any time comforting Jeremiah after he whines:

17 I did not sit in the circle of merrymakers, nor did I exult. Because of Thy hand upon me I sat alone, for Thou didst fill me with indignation.
18 Why has my pain been perpetual and my wound incurable, refusing to be healed? **Wilt Thou indeed be to me like a deceptive stream with water that is unreliable?**

WOW! Consider the arrogance of that question. He was basically asking God if He's going to let him down **AGAIN**. And honestly, isn't that what we do when we question His love and direction in our own lives?

After Jeremiah accuses God of being unreliable (a deceptive stream), which was incredibly self-centered, the Lord simply tells Jeremiah as well as you and me that when we question His love for us, we need to return to repentance before we can be the mouth of God. "We need to get past our navel gazing!" In other words, He asks us to focus on Him, not ourselves and our own discomfort. It's hard sometimes, but He makes us able. Like Jeremiah, we can repent and refocus on the Lord and His will.

<u>The Lord really can give us the ability to extract the precious from the worthless!</u> Trusting Him is an ability He freely gives us…we just have to learn to yield to Him.

## **THE KEY OF GOD'S APPROVAL**

What is God's testimony of you? Do you know? Have you asked Him?

You, like most people, probably assume that God's testimony of you isn't very good. Yes, we know that He loves us, but we think He loves us in spite of our frailties; which He does, but His love is bigger than we often realize.

Heb 11:1-2
1  Now faith is the assurance of things hoped for, the conviction of things not seen.
**2  For by it (FAITH) the men of old gained <u>approval</u>**.

Hebrews 11 is a chapter filled with stories about faith. I have to admit that I am more encouraged by those who even though they did not receive what they had faith for, were counted as faith-filled. And who approved of them? The Lord did! God's approval was on their lives. What could be better than that?

Heb 11:13-16
13  **All these died in faith, without receiving the promises**, <u>but having seen them and having welcomed them from a distance</u>, and having confessed that they were strangers and exiles on the earth.
14  For those who say such things make it clear that they are seeking a country of their own.

15  And indeed if they had been thinking of that country from which they went out, they would have had opportunity to return.
16  But as it is, **they desire a better country that is a heavenly one. Therefore <u>God is not ashamed to be called their God</u>**; for He has prepared a city for them.

Who, you might wonder, was impressed with their faith? It certainly was not the people around them who watched year after year as they suffered and died still hoping. And in the later part of this chapter, many suffered even worse things…

Heb 11:36-38
36  and <u>others experienced **mockings** and **scourgings, yes, also chains and imprisonment**.</u>
37  **<u>They were stoned, they were sawn in two</u>**, <u>they were tempted, they were **put to death with the sword**; they went about in sheepskins, in goatskins, being destitute, afflicted, ill-treated</u>
38  <u>men of whom the world was not worthy, wandering in deserts and mountains and caves and holes in the ground.</u>

I'm sure that absolutely no one who cruelly martyred them because of their faith was dazzled with them. Nobody on this earth may have even noticed their life of faith. They may have judged them foolish to die for somebody that they couldn't even see. But when we look at the following scriptures we can see who was delighted with their faith.

Heb 11:6
And **<u>without faith it is impossible to please Him</u>** for he who comes to God must believe that He is, and that He is a rewarder of those who seek Him.

Heb 11:39
And **<u>all these, having gained approval through their faith</u>**, did not receive what was promised,

As I was considering this scripture one day, the Lord asked me what I thought His testimony of me was. I've heard that when God asks you a question, you better realize quickly that you don't know the answer. So, my response was and is, "Oh Lord Jesus, I need your approval. Your opinion of me is the only one that really matters. But I must answer honestly,

"I don't really know."

Several years earlier, before I started praying about His approval, the Lord had asked me that same question. I asked Him to give me the answer. I wanted Him to show me. He gave me the following scripture.

Jer 17:5-8
5  Thus says the LORD, "Cursed is the man who trusts in mankind And makes flesh his strength, and whose heart turns away from the LORD.
6  "For he will be like a bush in the desert and **will not see** when prosperity comes, but will live in stony wastes in the wilderness, a land of salt without inhabitant.
7  "Blessed is the man who trusts in the LORD and whose trust is the LORD.
8  "For he will be like a tree planted by the water, that extends its roots by a stream and **will not fear** when the heat comes; but its leaves will be green, and it **will not be anxious** in a year of drought nor cease to yield fruit.

I felt that He was telling me that He does not curse me, but I could curse myself when I become my own god, trusting in my strength instead of the Lord's. Faithless, I had become like a tumbleweed in the desert, lacking adequate vision to see His provision for my life. Doubters are dry, dehydrated and merely existing without the living water flowing to, in and through them. The faithless are lonely in the wasteland. Because even though it is inhabited by others…they cannot see each other because they are consumed with their own lack of vision and understanding.

Conversely, the faith filled believers live by the water and it flows to, in and through them. And because of this living water, **they KNOW that the faithfulness of God will KEEP them no matter the circumstance**. They **will see** prosperity when it comes because they see the Lord! And HIS fruit ever endures. And did you notice that the scripture above says that the person of faith NEVER ceases to yield fruit? That's not natural… it is supernatural. And they know the satisfaction of being approved of by God.

One last note on this subject: In Genesis we see that Abraham did a few questionable things. He lied and said his wife was his sister. He tried to bring about God's provision with his own hands, giving birth to Ishmael.

But when God records these events for us in Hebrews 11, He tells the story with so much more grace than most of us would.

Hebrews 11:8-12
**8** By faith Abraham, when he was called, obeyed by going out to a place which he was to receive for an inheritance; and he went out, not knowing where he was going.
9 By faith he lived as an alien in the land of promise, as in a foreign *land*, dwelling in tents with Isaac and Jacob, fellow heirs of the same promise;
10 for he was looking for the city which has foundations, whose architect and builder is God.
11 By faith even Sarah herself received ability to conceive, even beyond the proper time of life, since she considered Him faithful who had promised.
12 Therefore there was born even of one man, and him as good as dead at that, *as many descendants* AS THE STARS OF HEAVEN IN NUMBER, AND INNUMERABLE AS THE SAND WHICH IS BY THE SEASHORE.

God looks at us His children with more grace than we can fathom. One step of faith to trust Him and He rewrites our biography. The Father looks at us with eyes of love because He uses His own Son as the lens, which means that we are approved of by God because we have Jesus as our Lord. What's better than that?

## THE KEY OF SEEING THE 'LIGHT'

Jn.12:35-50 was given to me in a dream. It was one of the most exact revelations that I have ever received. It was a mirror to me as TRUTH always is. My faithlessness was so stark to me in this dream that I woke up with a fear of the Lord that I have rarely experienced. He changed me. I started to realize what one of my favorite scriptures really means.

Rom 11:22
**Behold then the kindness and severity of God**; to those who fell, severity, but to you, God's kindness, if you continue in His kindness; otherwise you also will be cut off.

His warning was a great kindness to me and, as it turns out, also to the body I was attending at that time. It was a warning that we were all told to take notice of when the Lord allowed me to share it with them. <u>The severity came as a consequence of ignoring the admonition.</u>

I will split up the John 12:35-50 verses with an explanation for each section.

<u>The Dream</u>:

A service was being held at our church. As many people that normally attended were present. A man I didn't know was preaching with his wife standing next to him. He was a gifted teacher and she was very prophetic. They were an amazing team as they worked together seamlessly.

He was beginning to teach something new when his wife touched his arm. He immediately handed her the microphone and stepped back. She looked at us, and then she raised her voice and said, "There's a Light coming. Can you see it?" Everybody looked around with puzzled expressions wondering what she was talking about. Suddenly, a bright, almost blinding light filled the sanctuary. My husband and I dropped to the floor and started crying. I was face down, but I could hear several others crying as well.

I felt someone tapping on my shoulder. I looked up and saw the woman. She looked in my eyes and said, "This house is weak from unbelief!" I stared at her, puzzled. I looked over at our pastor who was also on the floor weeping, as if to say, 'Why are you telling me this. Tell him. He's the leader. He's the pastor, not me.' But I didn't speak that in the dream, I just thought it. Then she grabbed my shoulder, and even more intensely said, "This house is weak from unbelief!" When I made no response, she took both of my shoulders in her hands and firmly shook me and said, "You must warn them that this house is weak from unbelief."

And then in my dream I asked, "What's the scripture?" "John 12:35 to the end", was her reply. Then she started to walk back up on the stage. But I stopped her and said, "But I don't know what that scripture says." And she answered with a little bit of irritation, "Search it out!" Then she looked back at me and said, "Oh, Isaiah too." I called out to her, "Where in Isaiah?" But she just smiled and walked up the stairs to her husband and the dream ended.

I woke up and started to just roll over and go back to sleep. But the Lord seemed to yell in my head, "WRITE IT DOWN!" So I got up and wrote down the scriptures and went back to bed.

The next day I didn't look it up. It seemed so odd to me I thought that it was my imagination. The day after that I finally looked it up. Let's go through this a verse or two at a time.

John 12:35-36
35 Jesus therefore said to them, "For a little while longer the light is among you. Walk while you have the light, that darkness may not overtake you; **he who walks in the darkness does not know where he goes.**
36 **"While you have the light, believe in the light, in order that you may become sons of light**." These things Jesus spoke, and He departed and hid Himself from them.

The woman in the dream said that the Light is coming. In this scripture, Jesus refers to Himself as the Light. The Word of God is the light to our paths. Jesus is the living word of God. **Jesus is the Light of the Word of life for us.**

The darkness that will try to overtake us refers not only to sin, but also the consequences of sin, the very blindness that accompanies it. If we choose to walk in the darkness of practiced sin and faithlessness, we will not know where we are or where we are going. We will be lost. How can we find our way without His light?

We must choose to believe while He is available. This is time sensitive. When Jesus said it to His followers time was almost up! His time with them was drawing to a close.

John 12:37-38
37 But though He had performed so many signs before them, yet **they were not believing in Him**;
38 that the word of **Isaiah the prophet might be fulfilled, which he spoke, "Lord, who has believed our report?**

Is.53:1 And to whom has the arm of the Lord been revealed?"

Jesus performed miracles, but they would not believe.

## They CHOSE NOT TO BELIEVE.

Luke 18:8
"I tell you that He will bring about justice for them speedily. However, when the Son of Man comes, **will He find faith on the earth?**"

We can see in the two scripture verses above that both Isaiah and Jesus essentially ask the same question: Who will believe? Will Jesus find faith when He comes? No matter how He chooses to come, whether through a visitation, healing, miracles, manifestations or the whisper, He wonders if He'll find faith in us. This is where my heart broke. He is asking you… He's asking me. Will He detect the kind of faith that sees beyond earthly perceptions in me? Will He see that kind of faith in you?

John 12:39-41
39 For this cause **they could not believe**, for Isaiah said again,
40 "He has blinded their eyes, and He hardened their heart; lest they see with their eyes, and perceive with their heart, and be converted, and I heal them."
41 These things Isaiah said, because he saw His glory, and he spoke of Him.

First, they chose not to believe. **Then** we see that they/we are **unable to believe**. Does that alarm you? It sure alarms me! In my choice to be faithless in my own circumstances, I pave the way to my lack of ability to believe Him for my future. The consequence of this sin of unbelief is a poverty of vision, or blindness. In light of that terrible consequence I ask myself, "Can I afford to be unbelieving?" Can you?

Isa 6:10
"Render the hearts of this people insensitive, their ears dull, and their eyes dim, lest they see with their eyes, hear with their ears, understand with their hearts, and return and be healed."

It seems that God was dismayed at Israel's wickedness. But Isaiah had just seen a vision of the Lord. He had a revelation of the Glory of God. I think his heart must have been breaking under the weight of seeing Him. I'm sure that bringing the message of the revelation of the Glory of God overwhelmed him.

Isa 6:1-4
1 In the year of King Uzziah's death, **I saw the Lord sitting on a throne, lofty and exalted, with the train of His robe filling the temple.**
2 Seraphim stood above Him, each having six wings; with two he covered his face, and with two he covered his feet, and with two he flew.
3 And one called out to another and said, "Holy, Holy, Holy, is the LORD of hosts, the whole earth is full of His glory."
4 And the foundations of the thresholds trembled at the voice of him who called out

Isaiah must have felt inadequate to carry and articulate the majesty of God. The grief of their faithlessness must have broken him.

Isa 6:5
Then I said, "**Woe is me, for I am ruined**! Because I am a man of unclean lips, and I live among a people of unclean lips; for my eyes have seen the King, the LORD of hosts."

But even though he felt inadequate, he asked the Lord to send him with His message...a message of hope and holy fear of a glorious uncompromising God.

Isa 6:9
And He said, "Go, and tell this people: 'Keep on listening, but do not perceive; keep on looking, but do not understand.'

Heb 3:17-19
17 And with whom was He angry for forty years? Was it not with those who sinned, whose bodies fell in the wilderness?
18 And **to whom did He swear that they should not enter His rest, but to those who were disobedient**?
19 And so we see that **they were not ABLE TO ENTER BECAUSE OF UNBELIEF.**

In the above verses, we see that the disobedient ones were the unbelieving ones. These were **unable** to enter His rest.

And what is this 'rest'? It is the very resting-place of God; His abode... His dwelling in our hearts. An unhindered relaxation cushioned in trust. Rest is the freedom to fully know and be convinced of His goodness at all times.

Heb 4:1-2
1 Therefore, **let us fear lest, while a promise remains of entering His rest, any one of you should seem to have come short of it.**
2 For indeed we have had good news preached to us, just as they also; **but the word they heard did not profit them, because it was not <u>united by faith</u> in those who heard.**

We must unite the Word of God with faith or we will miss the point. How can we enter into all He has for us without faith? This is not a three-step program. This is a terrifying invitation to believe what He says. <u>Our lives</u>, as we have lived them, <u>will change</u>. We will be a peculiar people if we truly believe Him. That rest and peace is our greatest weapon against the enemy. Because the God of peace will soon crush Satan under our feet! <u>The confident rest of faith is impregnable to Satan</u>. He owns no weapon to defeat us when we live the peacefulness of true faith.

John 12:42-43
42 Nevertheless many even of **the rulers believed in Him, but because of the Pharisees they were not confessing Him**, lest they should be put out of the synagogue;
43 for **they loved the approval of men rather than the approval of God**.

I have never met anyone who at one point in their lives didn't care more about what people think of them than what God's testimony is of them. Many live lives of pleasing everyone but God. And in doing so, they are really just pleasing themselves with the praise of others. We rationalize that we do this or that to honor God. But in my own life, I can see it is often more satisfying to please people. The rewards are much quicker and more easily defined. I understand the rulers mentioned in the above verse. They long for safety more than they long to be ONE with Christ. This is a trap many fall into, of which few will repent. I want to want God's approval more than men's…I really want to want that…don't you?

John 12:44-50
44 And Jesus cried out and said, "He who believes in Me does not believe in Me, but in Him who sent Me.
45 "And he who beholds Me beholds the One who sent Me.

46 **"I have come as light into the world, that everyone who believes in Me may not remain in darkness.**
47 "And if anyone hears My sayings, and does not keep them, I do not judge him; for I did not come to judge the world, but to save the world.
48 **"He who rejects Me, and does not receive My sayings, has one who judges him; the word I spoke is what will judge him at the last day.**
49 "For I did not speak on My own initiative, but the Father Himself who sent Me has given Me commandment, what to say, and what to speak.
50 "And I know that His commandment is eternal life; therefore the things I speak, I speak just as the Father has told Me."

If we reject Him, we reject the Father. If we decide not to believe, we are rejecting life because He is life eternal. When we don't believe Him for our own lives, we choose to walk in the darkness of a faithless existence.

He is kind and severe. And His severe mercy asks again, "Will I find faith?" Will we see His light in times where only His light can illuminate our path? When the enemy threatens us in the dimness of difficult circumstances, can His light be found by us? He longs to lead us in the peaceful rest of trusting that He is faithful.

The Light is coming. Can YOU see Him?


## THE KEY OF TAKING TIME TO CHANGE OUR MINDS

Isa 62:10
Go through, go through the gates; **clear the way for the people**; build up, build up the highway; **remove the stones**, lift up a standard over the peoples.

Wade and I attended our previous church for almost thirty years. When the Lord made it clear that it was time to go, we suddenly had a lot of time on our hands. You see, my husband was an elder there for over twenty of those years. We were always concerned with other people's needs. We hadn't really taken much time to look inside our own hearts to see what we really needed or what was hiding inside of us.

When we left, people asked us where we were going and said that they might go there too. For that reason, and a few others, we decided to not become members of any church for approximately a year. We had watched people leave and take others with them and it was very painful. We just couldn't do that to our friends, the leaders that remained. So we visited other churches and stayed home a lot more than we ever could have before.

During that in-between time, I read an article by Steve Thompson. He is an amazing prophetic writer. I can always glean something valuable for my life from his insights. The article was called, 'Dealing with the Deadwood'. I'll briefly bring you up to speed.

Steve owned a piece of property that was only slightly developed. Much of it was covered with overgrowth, boulders and fallen trees. He needed more land for his family to be able to use. So it was time to clear the land. He found many things he was not expecting to find. Some of the fallen trees had rotted, making a home for several kinds of snakes to live and reproduce. He found huge boulders that could only be moved with large machinery and land that needed to be broken up, weeded and prepared in order to be useful. In the article he likened the downed trees, underbrush, boulders and other rocks as representing wrong ideas about God, others and himself. As he cleared the natural land, he realized that the land in his heart needed to be cleared as well. He took time off work to clear his land with an ever-present threat of torrential rain. Each day he worked hard to finish before the rain came. Miraculously, the Lord held back the rain until his work was finished.

During our year of 'resting', the Lord showed me many things in my own mind that needed to be cleared away so He could put more of my land to use. The Lord was attempting to change my mind. And when I think about it, He was probably trying to do that for quite awhile. I just was busying myself with other people's deadwood.

Changing my mind is just another way of saying that repentance was needed. Not that He was rooting out sin necessarily. But there were ideas I had hung onto that were obsolete or just plain wrong; ideas I had accepted independent of scripture that were just part of my culture of thinking. There were also things that God had said to do twenty years ago, but weren't relevant anymore. I wasn't seeing a new way but was struck in a rut.

We went through a process of allowing God to show us things inside of us, of which we were unaware. To list each thing would take too much space. The point is that it's important sometimes to stop what we are DOING and just BE with the Lord so He can clear out His property (you and me): Snakes of accusation and unloving judgments; rocks of hardhearted pride and unyielding ideologies. These are a few of the things that may need to be cleared away.

I'll give you one example: I always believed that God doesn't lead people **away**. I thought He only led people **to** some place. So when people left our church with no place to go, I judged them as not truly hearing from God. Now, where did I get that? Can I point to a scripture? Nope! In fact, the Lord told Abraham to go to a land that he didn't know. Here **I** was, moving **away** and not **to**, and being judged as I had judged others. It's a bitter thing to eat what you have wrongly served to others. But it is a lesson I'm not likely to forget.

The Lord was bringing up a wrong way of thinking (stronghold) almost every week. I would like to report that I immediately repented and was changed each time. But that's not true. I wrestled with God on several points. I was trying in my feeble way to convince God that this stronghold that I didn't want to give up was what He taught me. How stupid is that?!? Sometimes I think God, the Father, the Son and the Holy Spirit, look at us and smile and shake their heads. "Oh, they are so funny aren't they?" It's kind of like how we look at our children when they do silly things. You don't want to laugh at them, so you just smile and help them out. Then when you're alone with your spouse, you laugh and years later we tell the stories to their fiancée'.

In the article, Steve said the rain was held back. The delay of the rain was a blessing so that he could finish his task. As Christians, we often see rain as provision and blessing. At this writing, my husband and I still are waiting for release. It's difficult to wait for God to say yes. Most people are in the habit of listening for God to say 'NO', instead of waiting for Him to say yes. We know this rain of commissioning is a blessing we long for… but we must change our minds to see that the waiting is a blessing as well. There is still ground to be cleared before we get back to work. And if we move prematurely into new ground that is good but not the best, we forfeit the best rain…the perfect provision of God.

I think the waiting is the most significant lesson of all.  I realized that I saw my value in what we **did**, not who we were in the Lord.  <u>I found myself desiring a place of service so that others would find me valuable…and then I would be able to quantify my own worth</u>.  I didn't treasure the value that I had in the Lord for His sake only.  I wanted something to define me, like being an elder's wife.

I just read the previous paragraph and am embarrassed.  When I consider the value of my life from the Lord's perspective, the trivial things that I hope for make me feel sort of small.  I sing songs about God being all that I need but my heart wants more.  I want be useful in the eyes of His church.  But **I hear His quiet whisper saying that if I will let the Lord weed out this man-pleaser root, I will be so much freer and satisfied**.

See?  I have more ground to clear, more deadwood to gather up and discard.  I pray the Lord will delay the rain of commission until He is finished with the clearing-out process in me...though I'm sure that there will always be something to clear away as I move closer to Him. And at the same time, I feel sort of schizophrenic as I long for Him to release us to walk into the calling He has ordained.  I can see it in the distance.  It's a good and fertile land.  It is not without trial and hard work, but I am excited to make my way there in His timing.

## THE KEY OF KNOWING THE TIMES

1 Chr 12:32
And of the sons of Issachar, **men who understood the times, with knowledge of what Israel should do**, their chiefs were two hundred; and all their kinsmen were at their command.

We all have desires that we make known to God.  We ask for things to happen; like a new job; different people to come into our lives like spouses, children or friends; or we often ask for circumstances to change dramatically, like being healed or that we might move into a ministry.  And not quite as often, **many of us ask the Lord to tell us what He wants us to desire**.  I did that in the early '90's.  He deposited into my heart the desire to be a son (daughter) of Issachar.

I remember sitting in a group of women at a Bible study.  The question

*A Few Keys From the Pile*

of what we want from the Lord was asked. Each woman expressed her petition to the Lord. When it was my turn to share, I said that I wanted to be one of the daughters of Issachar. Everybody stared at me bewildered. I explained the tiny bit I knew at that point and realized I didn't really comprehend what it meant. I know that it is strange to want something when you aren't even sure what it means…but I did. So I figured I should search it out.

I still don't know enough about the Sons of Issachar, but I do know a little. The tribe of Issachar sent the least amount of men to the battle. Two hundred were sent and they were representative of the whole tribe with its varied skills. They were sort of the early day weathermen, like walking almanacs, knowing when to plant and when to harvest. Even though they were few in number, David needed them as much as the other tribes with greater strength. They were human calendars that could discern naturally and supernaturally, when to call the people to worship during appointed ceremonial times. They seemed to have their finger on the timing of God.

1. Esth 1:13
Then the **king said to the <u>wise men who understood the times</u>-- for it was the custom of the king so to speak before <u>all who knew law and justice</u>**,

The Sons of Issachar were statesmen and were referred to as princes having a firm grasp on politics and the state of the nation. They were <u>wise, noble leaders and obedient followers</u>.

2. Judg 5:15
"**And the <u>princes of Issachar</u> were with Deborah; as was Issachar, so was Barak; into the valley they rushed at his heels**; among the divisions of Reuben there were great resolves of heart.

The men of the tribe were hard workers, strong and industrious people given to strenuous labor.

3. Gen 49:14-15
14 "Issachar is a **strong donkey**, lying down between the sheepfolds.
15 "When he saw that a resting place was good and that the land was

148

pleasant, **He bowed his shoulder to bear burdens and became a slave at forced labor.**

This 'strong donkey' definition of the sons of Issachar explains a lot about my husband's and my life. Sons of Issachar are not the flamboyant race horses of the church. We do not have the short sprint in our minds and hearts. We are the stubborn burden bearers. You won't see us lined up against the gates snorting, kicking and anxious to start the race. NO, our heads are bowed; our hearts full of long suffering, our legs sturdy and our vision clear. **We live the marathon**. And even though we know this long suffering and lack of flashiness is what defines our faith, we still long to be found worthy of it. <u>Because that stubborn, sturdy faithfulness is what allows the Lord to trust us with His timing, and we count His trust as valuable as the most sparkling diamonds or the priceless treasure</u>. To be counted by God as trustworthy enough to know His timing is enormous. **I consider knowing the 'when' far more important than knowing the 'what'.**

The Sons of Issachar weren't the nation's soldiers. They labored at home and in the fields. And they were satisfied. They did, however, accompany Deborah and Barak (Judges 5:15) on the battlefield to <u>bring counsel regarding combat strategies</u> and emergencies.

OK. Now we know a little bit about the sons of Issachar. But let's try to translate that knowledge into today's vernacular. I think knowing the times means that they understood the timing of God, both natural and supernatural. Think about that for a minute. Their minds and hearts were in alignment with the willful and perfect timing of God.

How many times have you asked the Lord, "When?!?!" How long must I wait for 'due time'? When does the 'fullness of time' come? Even David cried out to the Lord, "HOW LONG?"

Ps 13:1-2
1 **How long, O LORD?** Wilt Thou forget me forever? **How long with Thou hide Thy face from me?**
2 **How long** shall I take counsel in my soul, having sorrow in my heart all the day? **How long** will my enemy be exalted over me?

Sounds pretty familiar to me!

Maybe I've whet your appetite for this 'knowing'. But the sons and daughters of Issachar today must be trusted friends of the Lord. Friends are far more intimate than servants. A friend can be trusted with the 'why' and the 'when' of things. He is not merely instructed to do this or do that. A friend is not simply an employee. Friendships may even develop into partnerships in the business. Not so for a mere servant/employee who works for a wage and goes home. How can the Lord be expected to give the delicate information of His timing to anyone that can't be fully trusted with helping to bear the burden first?

2 Pet 3:8-9
8 But do not let this one fact escape your notice, beloved, that **with the Lord one day is as a thousand years, and a thousand years as one day. 9 The Lord is not slow about His promise**, as some count slowness, but **is patient toward you, not wishing for any to perish but for all to come to repentance.**

In the above verses we see that His timing is a riddle. Without a revelation from Him, we can only guess. We also see that because of His great mercy and patience He sometimes delays. Not just regarding our ministries, but He is slow to promote as well. Premature promotion is a curse to the soul of the immature. The attention and demands of leadership or recognition can often short-circuit the plan of God in our lives. **We are ever in a hurry to live the promise but have difficulty in the process that guides us to that position.**

1 Pet 5:6-7
6 Humble yourselves, therefore, under the mighty hand of God, that He may exalt you at the **proper time,**
7 casting all your anxiety upon Him, because He cares for you.

Can we be trusted? As I ask the Lord to prepare me to understand the times, I often wonder if He is asking a question of me. "**How long must I wait for YOU to be trust-worthy?**" It is one thing to want to move in this wisdom, it is another thing to want it enough to prepare for it. I'm not sure but I think the preparation comes in being intimate with Him. Being like John and reclining at His breast. Close enough to hear His heart beating and feel the warmth of His breath. It is the quietness of friendship, the peacefulness of silence. Hearing the whisper because of the connection we share. Knowing you are safe with each other and that the bonds of love shared by us with Him are genuine.

<blockquote>
I want this kind of friendship with my Lord.
So I will continue to sit with Him and wait…ask…prepare.
</blockquote>

Gal 6:9
And let us not lose heart in doing good, for <u>in **due time** we shall reap if we do not grow weary</u>.

Two last notes of hope: **God spoke through a donkey!**

Numbers 22:28-33
28 And <u>the LORD opened the mouth of the donkey</u>, and she said to Balaam, "What have I done to you, that you have struck me these three times?"
29 Then Balaam said to the donkey, "Because you have made a mockery of me! If there had been a sword in my hand, I would have killed you by now."
30 The donkey said to Balaam, "Am I not your donkey on which you have ridden all your life to this day? Have I ever been accustomed to do so to you?" And he said, "No."
31 Then the LORD opened the eyes of Balaam, and he saw the angel of the LORD standing in the way with his drawn sword in his hand; and he bowed all the way to the ground.
32 The angel of the LORD said to him, "Why have you struck your donkey these three times? Behold, I have come out as an adversary, because your way was contrary to me.
33 "But the donkey saw me and turned aside from me these three times. If she had not turned aside from me, I would surely have killed you just now, and let her live.

**Jesus chose to make His triumphant entry on a donkey!**

Matthew 21: 2, 6-7
2 saying to them, "Go into the village opposite you, and immediately you will find a donkey tied *there* and a colt with her; untie them and bring them to Me.
6 The disciples went and did just as Jesus had instructed them,

7 and brought the donkey and the colt, and laid their coats on them; and He sat on the coats.

There are other examples of God's trust in the donkey…Even though we are stubborn and often foolish…The Lord trusts the heart of a strong and willing donkey! Burdens are meant to be born…but His yoke is easy as we rest in Him.

## THE KEY OF BEING A TRUE WORSHIPPER

Rev 22:17
And the **Spirit and the bride say, "Come."** And let the one who hears say, "Come."…

Heb 13:15
Through Him then, let us continually **offer up a sacrifice of praise to God**, that is, the fruit of lips that give thanks to His name.

When I think about worship, I think of passion, joy, exuberance, movement, listening and connecting with the heart of my Lord. He speaks love, peace, direction and encouragement among other things. Worship also makes me think of sacrifice and warfare. It's not about all the music; it's about our living what we believe.

Ps 2:11
Worship the LORD with reverence, and rejoice with trembling.

Ps 150:6
Let everything that has breath praise the LORD. Praise the LORD!

The Lord has challenged me to lead worship from my seat, in other words: my life. Now what does that mean? To me it means to be ever convinced that no matter what is happening, I am committed to pour forth worship. This is where the sacrifice comes into play. If we are to be the true worshippers of God, then we must choose to be wholly devoted to Him. We make the choice to put aside our need, to give Him what He desires. This is the challenge because we are all selfish and want to feel better. But we don't often realize that in giving Him our lives as an offering, He gives us more than we could have ever imagined.

Rev 15:4
"Who will not fear, O Lord, and glorify Thy name? For **Thou alone art holy; for all the nations will come and worship before Thee, for Thy righteous acts have been revealed.**"

Strong's Concordance
from 4314 and a probable derivative of 2965 worship (**meaning to kiss**, like a dog licking his master's hand); to fawn or crouch to, i.e. (literally or figuratively) **prostrate oneself in homage** (do reverence to, adore): KJV-- worship.

To worship the Lord is to minimize myself in my own eyes because in worship I see Him. Magnifying Him can be our most devoted response to His greatness. Acknowledging the 'bigness' of God, we give Him the only thing that is ours to give: praise and worship. His grace is amazing. His love is deeper, wider, higher and more awesome than we can understand. How can we resist falling at His feet in gratitude?

Francis Frangipane wrote about true worshippers in his book, The Three Battlegrounds. He likens their attitudes to the description of the Lord's attitude described in Is.53:4

Isa 53:4
Surely our griefs He himself bore, and our sorrows He carried; yet **we ourselves esteemed Him stricken, smitten of God, and afflicted.**

    In the 'Three Battlegrounds' (on pg. 72), the author tells us that God creates worshippers for His pleasure and that they (His worshippers) are pleased to give themselves to Him. He takes them through more pain and conflicts than other men, so they may seem 'smitten of God' as we see in the above scripture. Yet when they are crushed by difficulties and they yield to Him in worship in spite of their pain they exude a beautiful fragrance as a crushed flower would. So He is please to crush them because in their physical and emotional pain their faith and loyalty to the Lord grows ever stronger.

He is not saying that they are more like God. He is simply observing their devotion to the Lord in worship.

We were created for His pleasure. So when we yield to Him in worship, magnifying Him in word, song, dancing and in the testimony of our lives, He is pleased. Wow! If you are in pain at this moment and your suffering seems to be more than you can bear, take a moment to consider that He will turn aside and look at us in pleasure. He will actually stop what He is doing to see us in quiet or exuberant surrender. Just the thought of Him turning aside because we are able to please Him makes me want to worship Him even more. <u>It is within our power to actually delight the Lord.</u>

In the crushing, we can soar far above our circumstances and truly perceive Him. We can feel and see Him smile. But we have to choose it. This type of worship isn't for the nominal Christian…the ones merely surviving; the plastic Christian who looks good and is 'in the club' but is not the 'Bride'. This type of sacrifice can not be faked by one of the many.

I have experienced His pleasure in my pain. I am not saying that He is happy to allow the suffering, but He rejoices when we make Him bigger than the trial. The enemy wants to kill, steal and destroy. We can frustrate his efforts by looking for the Lord instead of the back door. When we choose to worship in the middle of the pain, I believe that we will see the Lord and He will allow us to smell the fragrance of the holy sacrifice of worship. I think that's when He celebrates and rejoices over us as in the verse below.

Zeph 3:17
"The LORD your God is in your midst, a victorious warrior. **<u>He will exult over you with joy</u>**, He will be quiet in His love, He will rejoice over you with shouts of joy.

(by permutation) guwl (gool); a primitive root; properly, **to <u>spin round</u> (under the influence of any violent emotion), i.e. usually rejoice,**

KJV-- be glad, joy, be joyful, rejoice.

In Zeph. 3:17 it says that He exults over you with joy. Did you know that this verse is saying that He spins or dances over you, rejoicing with powerful emotion? Let's not settle for dancing for Him, we can choose to dance with Him!

## **THE KEY OF THE LIVING FOUNTAIN**

Ps 36:7-9
7  How precious is Thy lovingkindness, O God! And the children of men take refuge in the shadow of Thy wings.
8  They drink their fill of the abundance of Thy house; and Thou dost give them to drink of the river of Thy delights.
9  For **with Thee is the fountain of life**; in Thy light we see light.

One morning I woke up early and began reading the word. It was bone dry. I kept reading in the hope that I would come across His heart as I read. But I couldn't find Him. So I closed the Bible and asked the Lord to hang out with me. At that very moment, He showed me something.

Before I describe what He showed me, I'd like to take this moment to write about intimacy. I've been told not to assume that anyone reading this has my same mind-set. So, when I consider intimacy with the Lord, my thoughts go to times of hearing His heart. He reveals His heart about many things. I love to hear His thoughts about my life, my family, church or anything really. But the most intimate times are when He shares with me His heart toward the world. He loves His church, His bride, but His heart seems almost broken over the condition of the world. They are lost and wander through life without hope and direction. His love for the lost seems almost desperate at times and I think that He longs to have company in His intercession for them.

The vision He gave me is about His heart to save our city. Portland, OR is very liberal politically and spiritually; Portland has a very strong Gay/Lesbian influence. All sin separates us from God and NO sin is worse than another, for all sin has consequences. At one time, the Northwest was known as the most unchurched region in the U.S. And whether that is still true or not, the atmosphere is still somewhat hostile to the Christian message. But still He longs to save each one that no one should perish.

Vision: I saw one of the fountains in downtown Portland. It was the one on the waterfront. It is the same elevation as the pathway. It had a flat surface with various openings within the spaces between the bricks where water springs up at different times in different ways to form varying springs. In the vision, people began to run through the springs and were refreshed. Some people watched for a while, and then left. Some people became marathon runners and carried a reproducing supply of the water with them as they ran. And some of the people became a part of the fountain.

I know that what I just wrote seems impossible because it seemed so to me. But as I took a closer look, the very stones from which the fountain waters sprung were living stones. Stones that were shapes of people flattened and fitted together. These people that became part of the growing fountain simply lay down and seemed at first glance to disappear, but they or the essence of what they were remained. The living water shot up from inside of them.

As I watched, the fountain continued to grow, first moving west then south. And finally this living fountain expanded to the north and east across the river. More and more people were refreshed, energized to bring the water to greater distances, and many chose to lie down and become a part of the hope for our city's new life.

John 4:13-14
13 Jesus answered and said to her, "Everyone who drinks of this water shall thirst again;
14 but whoever drinks of the water that I shall give him shall never thirst; but **the water that I shall give him shall become in him a well of water springing up to eternal life."**

My head tells me that with a liberal climate that would legalize assisted suicide, promote gay marriage and abortion rights, we may never win this city to the Lord. But, when I stop and let the Lord speak His heart to mine, I know that His desire will make a way. He loves the lost; He isn't concerned with politics and He isn't angry with unbelievers. He wants to take them into His family and make them safe. His goal is that we be one with Him and each other.

I need to adjust my thinking and join Him in His intercession for the lost in my family, city, country and world. I want to see with the eyes of faith. His desire that none perish is worth praying/fighting for.

KEY summarization: This last section regarding mercy, repentence, true worship, and the timing of the Lord are such big concepts, I'm sure I have barely scratched the surface of their meaning. But if we can catch the hope of His mercy. Or maybe lift our vision high enough to glimpse His heart in worship, or understand what His approval really feels like. Maybe then we can learn to extract the precious from th worthless, and freely see His light coming to illuminate our way, so we can become more like Him.

## CONCLUSION…

I would like to end this book with a word of encouragement to you, the reader. God has given each of us gifts and talents to be a benefit to Him, His church as well as the world. It is your job and mine to find out how we fit into His master plan. But please make NO mistake, we do FIT. Each of us has a unique perspective and role to play. To be completely fulfilled we must determine His assignment for us.

This last note to you is part of my journey to try to learn where I fit. The way that the Lord has taught me will be different from the way He instructs you. But that is what is so amazing about the way He teaches us… its like we are all being home schooled with our own unique curriculum which is tailored specifically to each of us.

I encourage you to receive His tutelage and seize everything He has to offer you. He longs to guide each of us toward Him and His grand design. I sincerely hope that you consider, collect and distribute the 'keys' He has given you.

## **MANY GIFTS / COUNTLESS KEYS**

He is the master artist. We are His canvas, His musical score sheet, or His blueprints yet to be finished. He is the ultimate inspired Creator. But even though His imagination is limitless, He asks us to be involved in His masterpiece. Though we are unskilled, He brings us into the process. What an amazingly patient instructor we have in our God.

So please, consider what He has in mind for you and your life. Will you be the sculpture of priceless marble or the multihued watercolor canvas on which the brilliant yellows bleed into the vibrant reds that give life to the bursting oranges of an erupting volcano in the blackest night? Maybe you will be the modern art piece that is made of the harshest rusted metal that is twisted and bent to form what is in the heart of the Creator. Perhaps life to you is like a sketch or charcoal drawing with the stark lines and shadows defining light and dark, hope and sorrow, truth and lie.

Search it out! Please understand your worth to the great Creator and search out the purpose for which you were made.

**Prov. 25:2**
It is the glory of God to conceal a matter, But the glory of kings is to search out a matter.

Early on in my own Christian journey, I completed several 'gift' tests. It was the 'thing' to do. Usually the teacher or leader giving the test would say something like: "You seem to have a prophetic gift…you should develop it." I had absolutely no clue how to do that! I didn't know much about the prophetic, but I figured that being prophetic was something that anyone could do. I took for granted that in its simplest form it was listening to God and saying whatever He wanted to be said or praying whatever He wanted to be prayed. So it seemed like the best way to hear Him would be to hang out with Him. You know, have a friendship with God.

Occasionally I read a book or heard a teaching about it, but not much more back then. I didn't want to have to do 'weird' things and call them prophetic. Some people seemed a little spooky to me or too contrived with the 'Thees' and 'Thous' and I wasn't really wild about being like that.

So I enrolled myself into God's school of the prophetic. There were four scriptures that kept my mind and heart busy for a long time. Frankly, these scriptures, as well as some others on this subject, still capture my imagination. They are the following:

1 Cor 14:3
But one who **prophesies speaks to men for edification and exhortation and consolation**.

Rom 12:6
And since we have gifts that differ according to the grace given to us, let each exercise them accordingly **if prophecy, according to the proportion of his faith**;

1 Cor 14:1
Pursue love, yet **desire earnestly** spiritual gifts, but **especially that you may prophesy**.

1 Cor 13:9
For we **know in part, and we prophesy in part**;

This was admittedly simplistic, but from the scriptures above I believed I only needed a few things to be effective in the prophetic. I needed to understand that building up the body through edification, exhortation and consolation was key. I needed to grow in faith to grow in a prophetic gift. Desire and developing a passion for hearing Him was important. And I felt no pressure to hear, do or say anything more than what He was giving me because I only get a part or a piece of the puzzle anyway.

As I grew in my relationship with the Lord, He started showing me different things about His nature so that I could represent Him better…just like everyone else that has made a commitment to Him. He started teaching me (and still is) how to see beyond my natural senses.

1 Sam 16:7
But the LORD said to Samuel, "Do not look at his appearance or at the height of his stature, because I have rejected him; for God sees not as man sees, for **man looks at the outward appearance, but the LORD looks at the heart**."

He taught me, and continues to teach me that it doesn't take any real prophetic ability to see sin. It's pretty hard to hide what's living in your heart. It is much more difficult to see the calling the Lord has for someone before it is realized. To see God's will for them and their future. It is a higher calling, in my opinion, to be willing to call forth the plans of God in someone and help them believe that God can and will partner with them to bring to pass what may seem impossible.

Eph 2:10
For we are His workmanship, **created in Christ Jesus for good works, which God prepared beforehand**, that we should walk in them.

Jer 6:27
"I have made you an assayer and a tester among My people, that **you may**

**know and assay their way."**

To analyze or assay what people are made of is more a process of seeing the precious than pointing out the worthless. People usually already know what is of questionable quality in their hearts. The accuser (Satan) reminds each of us daily. I believe when God challenged Jeremiah to become an assayer among His people, He wanted him to help the people in the refining of the gold that God was creating in them; to help someone begin that amazing excavation or mining process. Gold is a precious metal. It is a value to be sought and treasured, not ignored in pursuit of a less profitable search for wood, hay and stubble.

It's just so much more affirming to function in a Godly discernment than a spirit of critical cynicism, even though the later is much easier. I think the enemy of our souls loves it when Christian 'prophets' speak the indictments of the Accuser. Suspicion disguises itself as discernment far too often in the church, and to our shame we allow it sometimes, instead of judging it for what it is. Correctly judging a 'word' brings freedom to obey what is of God and to reject what isn't from His heart.

Many times the Lord has revealed the precious in people to me. And with that revelation I have often been required to guard or hold onto that word in secret and simply pray.

It is also important to guard prophetic words that are given to us by other believers. First, we should always scrutinize or judge the 'word'. If we are convinced that it is God's heart for us, we need to receive it. Should the *'word'* be incorrect, accusation or flattery, we should reject it. Personally, I never assume that any 'word' that I receive for or from anyone is automatically 'right'. And I expect everyone I present with a 'word' to go ask 'Dad' (Father God) about it. We should NEVER assume that any 'word' is automatically from God…I don't care how gifted the person appears to be. It's foolish…or frankly just plain irresponsible not to check with 'Dad' first.

I was given a 'word' for a friend. I asked 'Dad' and received it. The prophetic person who delivered it is internationally known and well respected. It had to do with the kind of person he would be. A leader was his calling in part, but first he would resist the Lord and 'kick against the bricks', but that one day he would be a Joshua in the house of God.

For years this word made no sense to me, because I 'assumed' that God meant the Joshua in the book of Joshua. Then many years later I was reading Zechariah.

Zech 3:1-7
1 Then he showed me Joshua the high priest standing before the angel of the LORD, and Satan standing at his right hand to accuse him.
2 And the LORD said to Satan, "The LORD rebuke you, Satan! Indeed, the LORD who has chosen Jerusalem rebuke you! **Is this not a brand plucked from the fire?"**
3 Now Joshua was clothed with filthy garments and standing before the angel.
4 And he spoke and said to those who were standing before him saying, "Remove the filthy garments from him." Again he said to him, **"See, I have taken your iniquity away from you and will clothe you with festal robes."**
5 Then I said, "Let them put a clean turban on his head." So they put a clean turban on his head and clothed him with garments, while the angel of the LORD was standing by.
6 And the angel of the LORD admonished Joshua saying,
7 "Thus says the LORD of hosts, 'If you will walk in My ways, and if you will perform My service, then you will also govern My house and also have charge of My courts, and I will grant you free access among these who are standing here.

When I read the above scripture, the Lord spoke to me: '**THIS** is the Joshua I was talking about".

The other Joshua didn't make sense to me because he never walked away from God. My friend chose to do that…but he **WILL** be a brand plucked from the fire!

I guard this word to this very day, longing and praying that the Lord will bring it to pass.

Sometimes the Lord has required me to guard words for His people for a month, six months, a year, and two years. And for one person I have carried a word for over twenty years so far…this same word I still carry in faith, looking forward to the day that He brings it to pass. I consider this a great privilege.

In one instance, I was awakened by the Lord for two years to pray for someone I hardly knew. He did not wake me up every night, but it was at least twice a week. I remember crying without understanding. I wondered why I was so moved since I hardly knew her. But God knew her and missed her deeply.

Another time I had a vision of a man I knew walking in water up to his ankles.

Ezek 47:3-5
3 When the man went out toward the east with a line in his hand, he measured a thousand cubits, and **he led me through the water, water reaching the ankles**.
4 Again he measured a thousand and **led me through the water, water reaching the knees**. Again he measured a thousand and **led me through the water, water reaching the loins**.
5 Again he measured a thousand; and it was a river that I could not ford, for the water had risen, enough **water to swim in**, a river that could not be forded.

The Lord told me that He was going to give this man a wife. My job was to pray for him so that he would know her when she came.

On a personal note, it was very hard not to tell this man about God's wedding plans for him. He had been divorced from his first wife for many years, but he still wore the ring. He told me more that once that he wished that he was still married. And even though she had remarried, he continued to wear the ring. I knew God's plans for him would bless him. And I wanted him to know that the Lord cared deeply about how he felt and that God was making a way for him to have the desire of his heart. But, the timing of telling him was not my choice. The choice of when to share the word with him fell to the One who gave the word, not to me. It would have to wait until the Lord said that he was ready to hear it. Our heavenly Dad knows best.

The Lord gave me the above Ezek. scripture for him and said that when the water reached his waist and he began to swim, I was to tell him what God had shown me. I did not have permission to tell him before he was swimming. As I prayed for him the vision changed. After about ten months, the water had risen to his knees. After one and a half years, the water had risen almost to the top of his legs. In a little over two years, the water was at his waist. Two months after that, he was swimming and I told him that it was time to find his wife and get married. He told me he had met someone and was getting to know her. He asked her to marry him several months later. They are a wonderful couple…just perfect for each other. Isn't God smart, kind and wonderful!

The Lord has also given me correction for some people. This is very delicate. He had to instruct me first.

God is very sensitive about how His children are corrected. He doesn't want them to be wounded in any way. If you are a parent, you will probably remember a time when one of your children was corrected in an unkind way. You probably felt angry and you may have wanted to protect your son or daughter from the person who hurt them. Our heavenly Father is even more protective of us. He doesn't want us to be 'careless' toward His kids. We need to see others as His children and be careful with their minds, hearts and feelings when we bring difficult instruction to them.

Along with examples of poorly given correction, He helped me to remember what it felt like when people blessed our kids. How it was more of a gift to us than a gift given directly to us. Any parent knows that when someone loves your children, it means more than anything else they could do. We have experienced this with both of our kid's spouses. Maranda married a man who loves and cares for her so sweetly that we are thrilled that the Lord gave him to her. He is exactly what she needed and wanted. And Jered's wife is perfect for him. She knows him completely and makes a way for him. She is a king maker for our son and we are truly grateful to the Lord for making her a part of our family.

Our heavenly Father loves us as our true Father. And when we bless or wound another one of His children, it touches Him. He experiences joy when we bless each other. And it is painful for Him when we hurt another one of His children. So I try to see one of my kid's faces when I am required to bring a rebuke… with the hope that the kindness of the Lord will lead them to or grant them repentance.

Rom 2:4

Or do you think lightly of the riches of His kindness and forbearance and patience, not knowing that **the kindness of God leads you to repentance**?

2 Tim 2:24-25
24 And the Lord's bond-servant must not be quarrelsome, but be kind to all, able to teach, patient when wronged,
25 with **gentleness correcting** those who are in opposition, if **perhaps God may grant them repentance** leading to the knowledge of the truth,

I look forward to learning more about this gift of prophecy. Since we are instructed to desire it, and that we all have a 'part' to play in God's design, His masterpiece. We can all learn to be better exhorters.

1 Cor 14:31-32
31 **For you can <u>all</u> prophesy** one by one, so **that all may learn and all may be exhorted;**
32 and the **spirits of prophets are subject to prophets;**

I don't think that prophecy has to be mysterious. People exercising a gift of prophecy don't have to be 'weird', do things that are out of order, or promote themselves with loud pronouncement of 'Thus says the Lord'. He is unfailingly true so we can be like Him...trustworthy, especially in prophetic wisdom, since it comes directly from Him.

I personally think that every gift has the element of the prophetic. How else do servants, administrators, givers and leaders know exactly what, when and how to do something at the exact time it is needed.

The Lord, Our awesome Creator, is ever composing, constructing and painting the artwork of you and me. New designs, new color choices blending and contrasting to fashion a distinctive point of view. After all, WE ARE HIS to mold as He wills. We are His workmanship created for good works in Christ.

Pursue Him…but look also to see what He holds in His hands for you. The gifts He will pour through you for others. The tools He desires to implement in you for His grand design. We are works in progress… enjoy the expansion of His infinite imagination! Let yourself consider the possibilities as well as all of the 'keys' He is giving you.

In this last section, I have attempted to convey some small insight into deeper things. I am heartened by His patient instruction to me and hopeful for more understanding.

Most importantly,<br>
INTIMACY WITH HIM IS THE ULTIMATE KEY<br>
that unlocks every door between us.

There is always more to be discovered, because He has no end. And I am aware that what I don't know could fill several libraries. Still, this is a beginning into a lifelong expedition with my Lord.

1 Cor 2:9-10
9 but just as it is written, <u>"Things which eye has not seen and ear has not heard, and which have not entered the heart of man, all that God has prepared for those who love Him."</u>
10 **For to us God revealed them through the Spirit; for the Spirit searches all things, even the depths of God.**

He longs to take us for a journey through His 'depths'. If we are willing to lay aside the entanglements encumbering us, we can travel with Him into many mysteries. Imagine…exploring the depths of God with the Holy Spirit as our personal guide!

These have been just a few keys from the pile.<br>
I hope that you enjoyed reading them. And I hope to hear about the keys that He has given you.

Gayle M. Nelson

## ACKNOWLEDGMENTS

I must take a moment to thank some people who have helped me with the writing of this book.  My husband is almost a co writer and his guidance has assisted me in making this far more well rounded than if I had tried to write it on my own.  Kim Maricle gave this it's final edit and I really trust and appreciate her help.  And last but certainly not least, Jim Gullett made this project of mine come to pass.  I can honestly say that it would not have happened without his help.  THANKS EVERYBODY!!!!

Gayle M. Nelson

*A Few Keys From the Pile*

Gayle M. Nelson

www.ingramcontent.com/pod-product-compliance
Lightning Source LLC
Chambersburg PA
CBHW031444040426
42444CB00007B/971